Government Debt in International Financial Markets

A publication of the Graduate Institute of
International Studies, Geneva

Government Debt in International Financial Markets

Dirk Morris

 Pinter Publishers, London and New York

© Dirk Morris, 1988

First published in Great Britain in 1988 by
Pinter Publishers Limited
25 Floral Street, London WC2E 9DS

British Library Cataloguing in Publication Data

A CIP catalogue record for this book is available from the British Library

ISBN 0-86187-994-5

Library of Congress Cataloging-in-Publication Data

Morris, Dirk.
  Government debt in international financial markets / Dirk Morris.
    p. cm. -- (A Publication of the Graduate Institute of International
    Studies, Geneva)
    Bibliography: p.
    Includes index.
    ISBN 0-86187-994-5 : $45.00
    1. Debts, Public. 2. Debts, Public--United States. I. Title.
  II. Series: Publications de l'Institut universitaire de hautes études
  internationales, Genève.
  HJ8030.M57 1988
  336.3'4--dc19   88-22695 CIP

Filmset by Mayhew Typesetting, Bristol, England
Printed by Biddles of Guildford Ltd.

List of Tables

List of Figures

Acknowledgements

This book could not have been produced without the financial support of the Reserve Bank of Australia. I wish to thank all those at the Bank who encouraged me to go overseas to study; Peter Jonson and Jeffrey Carmichael were particularly influential in guiding me back into the academic world. Generous financial support at the publication stage was also provided by the Swiss Bank Corporation, the University of Geneva and the Graduate Institute of International Studies.

I am most deeply indebted to Hans Genberg, who has provided me with many ideas, constant support, useful criticism and a stimulating work environment. Others have also contributed greatly to my research: Alexander Swoboda; John Cuddy; and Uli Camen have all played an important role — in forming my thoughts, improving my skills as an economist, and commenting directly on my work. I must also thank Svein Andresen, Luc Everaert, Ethan Weisman, Francisco Nadel-de-Simone, Vera Gowlland and Anne-Marie Gulde, all of whom read and commented on earlier versions of the manuscript.

I have greatly benefited from the comments received at seminars I have given, both at the Graduate Institute of International Studies and at the Swiss National Bank. I would like to thank those who organized and those who attended the seminars.

Finally, I want to thank my family, who have been extremely tolerant of my long hours absent from home. I am especially indebted to my wife, Lisa, who also typed many of the earlier drafts and who has helped greatly in editing and proof-reading.

Foreword

The evolution of exchange rates and current account imbalances between major industrialized countries, in particular the United States, Japan and Germany, during the past ten years have presented several major puzzles for academic economists and significant challenges for policy makers. The sharp and prolonged appreciation of the U.S. dollar relative to both the DM and the Yen in the early eighties followed by the equally sharp depreciation since 1985 has proved difficult to explain in terms of what mainstream economic models refer to as 'fundamental' variables such as inflation differentials, current account developments, interest rates etc. Frustration with this inability to account for the massive swing in the external value of the dollar has led some economists to provide 'explanations' by referring to speculative bubbles that expand and eventually burst, and to point to the misalignment of currencies that may result from 'excessive' international mobility of financial capital. Similarly, the length of time it has taken for the current account deficit of the United States to show some improvement despite the sharp depreciation of the dollar has called into question a number of widely held views concerning the link between exchange rate movements and trade.

This study by Dirk Morris takes up the challenge introduced by the events in the seventies and eighties and proposes an explanation of these events that emphasizes fiscal policy and the evolution of government debt. According to this explanation, the puzzles associated with the swings in the dollar and the persistence of the external deficit of the United States can to a large extent be explained by differences in fiscal-monetary policy mixes pursued in the United States on the one hand and Germany and Japan on the other. What differentiates Morris' explanation from previous studies emphasizing fiscal policy is the attention given to the dynamic effects of such policies through their impact on government debt. It has often been suggested that the current-account and exchange-rate developments in the eighties cannot adequately be accounted for by references to fiscal policy because the turn-around of the dollar in 1985 did not coincide with a simultaneous turn-around of the US fiscal deficit. Morris shows that if the impact of fiscal deficits on government debt is taken into account, and if the influence of this debt on interest rates, exchange rates and current accounts are evaluated, it is possible to provide an integrated explanation of the evolution of these variables.

Any explanation that emphasizes the evolution of government debt must face up to the challenge posed by the so-called Ricardian Equivalence hypothesis according to which it is immaterial how a given budget deficit is financed, be it through tax increases or public sector borrowing. Those who believe that this hypothesis is valid have disputed any role for fiscal policy as an explanation of recent movements in real interest rates and real exchange rates. The empirical tests contained in Part II of Morris' study reject the Ricardian Equivalence hypothesis. In contrast to many previous studies that have produced results more favorable to the hypothesis, Morris emphasizes the need to adopt an international perspective in view of the increasing integration of the world's capital markets. He shows that treating each country as if it were isolated from the rest of the world, when in fact it is not, might erroneously lead an investigator to accept the Ricardian view.

The policy implications of the study are far-reaching. If fundamental economic forces can explain interest-rate, exchange-rate, and current-account developments there is no need to rely on special factors such as destabilizing speculation. Policy measures like capital controls then become unnecessary. The emphasis on government debt as a critical variable instead means that the conduct of fiscal policy must be given special attention in any strategy aiming at reducing international conflict over exchange rates and trade imbalances. In particular it ought to be at the center of any policy coordination undertaken as a result of G-7 negotiations. Morris shows that exchange-rate targeting through interventions in foreign exchange markets will be very difficult, and may even be destabilizing, if it is not accompanied by harmonization of fiscal policies. Furthermore, his results indicate that a major reason for the US current account problem has been that country's fiscal deficit and growing public debt. Consequently, the most direct way to solve the problem is not to try to manipulate exchange rates but to deal directly with the fiscal imbalance in the United States. Viewed in this light, the persistence of the external balance of the United States is no longer a puzzle but reflects the political difficulties in reducing the public sector deficit.

As this brief foreword has attempted to indicate, the present study deals with subjects that have important implications both for theoretical developments and for policy making. For anyone interested in international macroeconomics, it offers a blend of theoretical inquiry and applied empirical work that is to be commended. Academics and policy makers alike will find it a valuable source of information; analysis, and policy conclusions.

Hans Genberg
Graduate Institute of International Studies

Chapter 1

Introduction

Aims

The period since the mid-to late 1970s has provided economists interested in the effects of budget deficits and debt with an unprecedented case study. After having fallen to post-war lows in the early 1970s, the level of real government debt has since expanded rapidly in nearly all the major industrial economies. Even more interestingly, the pattern of expansion has been highly uneven. In Japan and Europe the most dramatic expansion began almost immediately after the first oil shock and has only recently begun to slow. In contrast, the United States has seen its government debt outstanding accelerate rapidly since 1982 as the Reagan deficits, combined with Volcker's unaccommodating monetary policy, raised the debt to GNP ratio dramatically.

Sustained borrowing to finance public spending is, of course, not a new phenomena. There are, however, a number of factors making the recent experience unique. In the first place, sustained debt financing has normally occurred during periods of war or as a result of major and prolonged depressions. In contrast, the current expansion of US debt has largely been the result of substantial tax cuts, rather than an increase in recession- or war-associated expenditures. Second, during the previous comparable episodes of major real debt financing (the two world wars and the great depression) the world economy, and particularly financial markets, were extensively controlled and regulated via direct government intervention. Since the early 1970s, with the floating of exchange rates, the removal of most internal and external controls on financial markets, and the improvements in communications technology, governments issuing debt face a totally different environment. Public sector financial instruments must compete directly with other domestic instruments and, even more importantly, with financial instruments from throughout the world. Given this situation, economists now have a near perfect chance of examining how deficit financing influences freely operating domestic markets and how such effects might spill over and impact on other countries, and international financial markets in general.

It is, therefore, not surprising that economists have reopened the old debates on financial crowding-out and the Ricardian Equivalence Theorem and that the journals are currently awash with articles on the actual and likely future effects of US budget deficits. At the same time, this recent literature has (with few exceptions) ignored the open economy aspects of the deficit issue. The contribution that the present study hopes to make to the literature is to provide a detailed examination of the debt neutrality hypothesis under the assumption of integrated international financial markets.

Two different, although related, approaches are employed. The first approach focuses on the world economy as a whole. In this framework closed economy models can be used to examine the impact of world policy variables on world financial markets. By building up the closed world economy from the sum of the individual open economies that make up the world, it is possible to highlight the weaknesses introduced by using the closed economy model to analyse the individual small or medium-sized economy. This approach also allows for substantial simplification of the theoretical models and the econometric techniques needed to make strong tests of the Ricardian Equivalence Theorem. In particular, it allows one to avoid the complex issues of transmission and multi-country linkages, without violating the assumption of asset market integration and capital mobility. The second approach is both more ambitious and more tentative. It is based on the multi-country framework in which issues of transmission and asymmetries (that is, differences) are crucial. The differences between economies show up most importantly in such variables as exchange rates and current accounts, and these will become the major focus of attention in the multi-country world.

The two approaches correspond directly with the two key, but inter-related, questions addressed in the policy co-ordination debate: the first concerns the appropriate levels for the world policy instruments, and the second, the appropriate distribution of the instruments between the individual economies. Given this correspondence, it is hoped that the results of the empirical work can be applied to the question of fiscal policy co-ordination; in particular, to the possible role of fiscal policy in stabilizing real exchange-rate fluctuations, and smoothing average world interest rates.[1]

Structure

The book is divided into two parts. The first examines the theoretical issues, beginning with the notions of intertemporal accounting and Ricardian equivalence. The intertemporal theory of fiscal deficits has recently been extended to the open economy framework and the contribution of this literature is outlined. Chapter 3 concentrates on the standard income-expenditure models of macroeconomics. The emphasis is on deriving empirically testable conclusions about deficits and debt. This is done in both the closed and open economy models, to be consistent with the dual approach to be taken in the empirical work. Results from both the income-expenditure and intertemporal models will be compared and contrasted.

Part II is devoted to testing the key empirical hypotheses developed in Part I. It commences, in Chapter 4, with a review of the existing empirical literature. Chapter 5 avoids the complexities of a multi-country world by assuming asset market integration and aggregating the major industrial economies into a 'world' average. Reduced-form interest-rate equations can then be used to test for debt neutrality, without incorporating complex international financial linkages. Chapter 6 explores the more complex issues of international financial linkages by estimating a complete two-country model. Simulation analysis is used to illustrate the dynamic response of financial markets to deficit shocks, in both the US and non-US blocs. Chapter 7 attempts to bring together some policy conclusions from the two alternative empirical approaches. Appendix A provides a detailed listing of all data sources. Appendix B explores empirically the dynamics of capital accumulation in the world economy framework.

Before diving into this largely technical study, it is worth briefly reviewing some selected stylized facts that have been the motivation for the book. This will help to keep the following abstract theory in perspective, as well as providing the reader with a better feel for the size of financial market upheavals that have characterized the economic history of the 1970s and 1980s.

Background

International financial markets

Perhaps the most outstanding economic feature since the 1960s has been the enormous upheavals that have taken place in international financial markets. The 1960s witnessed the removal of many institutional barriers to the growth of international capital markets and, along with technological breakthroughs in the communications field, the resulting rise in capital mobility helped to undermine the relatively stable fixed exchange-rate system that had been established after World War Two. Expectations that a floating exchange-rate system would provide more financial market stability, by harnessing speculative forces, have not been fulfilled.

Figure 1.1 plots the percentage deviations of the real effective US dollar

Figure 1.1 The real effective US dollar.

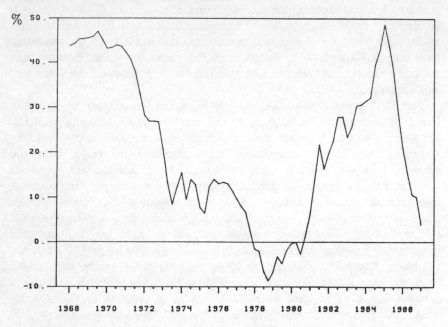

Sources: see Appendix A.

exchange rate (from a 1980 base) for the period 1968 to 1987:1. Bilateral nominal exchange rates for the G7 members have been deflated using consumer prices and weights are based on relative size (using GNP). The figure provides an example of the huge cyclical variations that have occurred in foreign exchange markets since the beginning of the floating exchange-rate period; swings that have far exceeded the movements in relative consumer prices.[2] The appreciation of the dollar between 1980 and the first quarter of 1985 was around 50 per cent; it has since been followed by a depreciation of similar size (in an even shorter period of time). The only period of relative stability is for the year 1987 (not shown due to data limitations). That year was also the first in which central banks actively returned to the foreign exchange markets in order to slow the rising instability that reached dramatic levels during 1985 and 1986.

The growing instability has not been confined to foreign exchange markets, but is reflected in all aspects of financial market operations, including money, stock and bond markets. As one indicator of this, Figure 1.2 presents an average of the major industrial countries' government bond yields. The yield is on long-term bonds and is in both nominal terms and real terms (that is, adjusted for inflationary expectations). The

Figure 1.2 Real and nominal world interest rates.

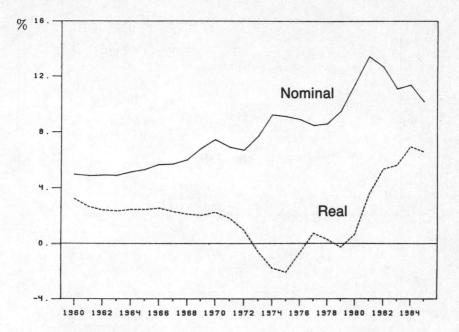

Sources: see Appendix A.

real rate is the nominal rate less a centred three-year moving average of inflation. Because bonds are long-term, even small movements in this interest rate represent large changes in the real capital value of the bonds.

Two points stand out from this figure. First, the increased variability in interest rates occurred around the same time as the breakdown in the nominal exchange-rate system. Second, the rise in variability has been present in both real and nominal rates.[3] In terms of the general pattern displayed, it is interesting to note that the 1970s was a period of very low real rates, compared to the 1960s and especially to the 1980s. The 1980s has been a period of record high real interest rates by any measure. There appears to be no direct correlation between the pattern of exchange-rate movements and the average world interest rates shown. This is perhaps not surprising as it is likely to be differential movements in country interest rates that would be linked with exchange-rate movement, rather than the averages shown above.

To get some idea of the degree of financial market correlation across countries, Figure 1.3 plots the real long-term bond rate for the United States and an average of the other G7 countries for the years 1971–86.[4] Although the figure indicates that the major countries have all tended to

Figure 1.3 US and non-US real interest rates.

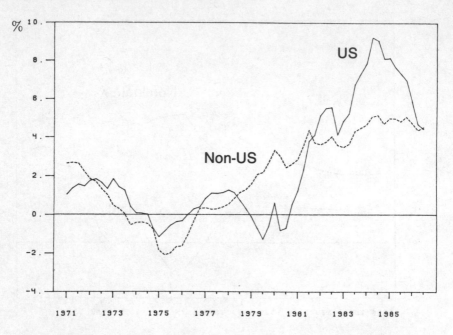

have lower real interest rates in the 1970s and relatively high real rates in the 1980s, it also points to substantial divergences in rates between the United States and the non-US countries shown at certain points in time. In particular, over much of the 1980s, the US real interest rate has been substantially higher than rates in the other major countries.[5] Similarly, there have been periods during the 1970s when rates in the United States have deviated sharply from those in the other OECD countries.

The divergence in financial markets between the United States and non-US countries has not only been reflected in financial prices, but has also shown up in shifting stocks of financial instruments across countries. Associated with the higher returns on US assets since 1980 has been a flood of foreign capital into US financial markets. These flow imbalances are readily seen in Figure 1.4, where the current account positions of the United States and the non-US bloc are shown.[6] Until the early 1980s the current account imbalances between the major industrial economies had been relatively minor and never very prolonged. In contrast, since around 1983 the US current account deficit has soared to nearly $40 billion dollars a quarter, or around $150 billion dollars a year. At the same time, the non-US countries have moved to a substantial surplus. This imbalance shows no signs of disappearing in the near term. The major implication of this imbalance in goods and capital flows is that US citizens are running

Figure 1.4 US and non-US current accounts.

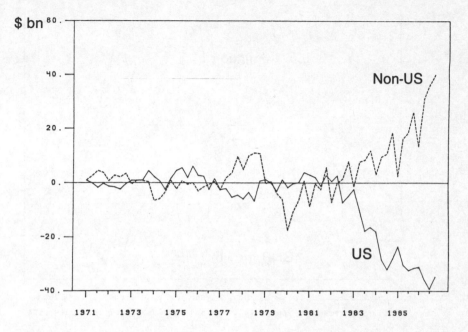

down their stocks of foreign assets, while the non-US bloc is accumulating large amounts of US dollar assets. Indeed, the United States has now become the world's largest debtor, and is likely to remain so for the foreseeable future.

Such massive shifts in the location and ownership of financial assets makes it difficult to believe that financial markets are being driven only by short-run speculative behaviour. Why would one of the richest and most capital-intensive countries in the world all of a sudden go into debt to the rest of the world to the tune of what may exceed $500 billion by the end of the decade? The next section presents some data on a few likely real factors that may be driving the major cycles in international financial markets.

International fiscal policy

One of the primary aims of this book is to try and relate the above financial market disturbances to real economic imbalances (particularly fiscal imbalances), both at the world level and across countries. It seems likely that the large cyclical swings in financial markets since the early 1970s are not solely a result of the change in exchange-rate regime and the

Figure 1.5 World economic growth and inflation.

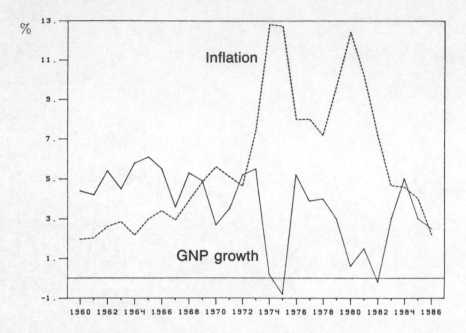

increasing sophistication of financial institutions.[7] The question that must be answered is, what real variables could have induced such massive swings in real interest and exchange rates and international asset stocks?

Figure 1.5 provides the real GNP growth rate of the major industrial economies, along with the rate of inflation. The figure confirms that variability in both economic growth and inflation has been much more pronounced throughout the 1970s and 1980s than in the 1960s. The recessions of 1974–5 and 1980–2 were much more severe than anything experienced during the 1960s. Similarly, the inflation rate has also been much more unstable since the early 1970s than it was during the 1960s. At the same time, the increased goods-market imbalances do not seem that much more acute to warrant the growing financial market instability outlined above. In particular, there seems to be little in goods markets to explain the dramatic swings in interest and exchange rates since 1983, when world economic growth and inflation were relatively stable.

One possible explanation for the growing instability in financial markets is that, as these markets become more sophisticated and less restricted, they are more able to play a shock-absorbing role. Large swings in financial markets may, in fact, help to smooth out exogenous external disturbances that would have otherwise altered the private sector's behaviour in goods markets by even more than indicated in Figure 1.5. What are the

Figure 1.6 US and non-US debt to GNP ratios.

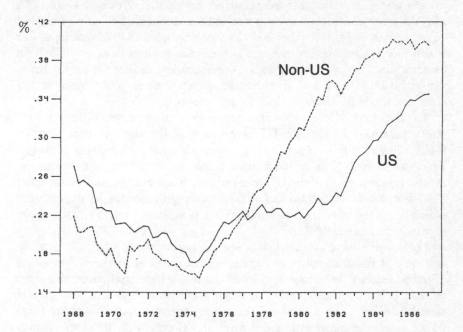

external exogenous shocks that financial markets may have been responding to? The most obvious, and well discussed, are the three oil shocks.[8] These upset world consumption and savings balances and required massive flows of funds across countries. There are also other shocks stressed in the literature, such as productivity shocks and monetary policy shocks, which may have contributed to the rise in financial market instability. Finally, another source of disturbance may have come from erratic government fiscal policy.

One measure of the dramatic changes in fiscal policy over the recent period is shown in Figure 1.6. It presents the US debt to trend GNP ratio and an average ratio for the non-US bloc. For nearly all industrial countries, debt fell sharply during the 1960s and especially the early 1970s. In most countries, debt levels began rising after the first oil shock and have continued on an upward trend since the early 1970s. Current levels are not extremely high in most of the large countries by historical standards. However, as already pointed out above, the previous large rises in government debt have almost always been short-lived and associated with wars or major depressions.

Figure 1.6 also suggests that the rise in world government debt has not been solely the result of US fiscal frivolity. Indeed, over the entire floating-rate period it is the non-US countries that have contributed most to the rise in world debt. Another point from the graph is the uneven rise in debt across countries that has occurred during the 1970s and 1980s. The non-US countries reached a low point in their debt to GNP ratio of around 15 per cent in 1974. Debt then rose very rapidly until 1980 (doubling), after which time it continued to rise at a slower pace until peaking in 1985:1. In contrast, the US debt to GNP ratio rose much less during the period up to the early 1980s (around 5 percentage points); since which time it has accelerated rapidly to more than 34 per cent.

The rises in debt levels have also been used to finance very different fiscal policy packages. In the non-US bloc much of the rise has been used to finance higher public expenditures, especially on social support schemes. This was partially true in the United States in the 1970s, but during the 1980s a major portion of the US debt expansion has been to finance tax cuts. The United States has also had a major reorganization of its expenditure policies; giving priority to military expenditure, rather than social expenditures, since 1980.

The above selected stylized facts are suggestive of a strong link between government financial policy and international financial markets. The surge in public sector debt outstanding in all the major industrial economies since the late 1970s matches closely the sharp and sustained rise in real interest rates.[9] Similarly, the timing of the recent growing imbalances in fiscal stance across the major economies correlates closely with the cross country imbalances in financial markets. These are the issues that are explored in the following chapters, both on a theoretical and empirical level.

Notes

1. These twin goals of policy co-ordination were first made clear at the 1987 IMF/World Bank annual meeting by the US Treasury Secretary, James A. Baker III. He explicitly called for the use of a global average target (a commodity price index) to help guide international policy co-ordination.
2. The book will be concerned with the medium-term fluctuations in financial variables. No attempt is made to explain very short-term volatility in financial prices.
3. These conclusions are not dependent on the type of interest rate chosen, or the measure of inflationary expectations used to obtain a real rate.
4. For all the remaining figures presented in this chapter (and throughout the book), average data are obtained by using GNP based weights. Some discussion of appropriate weighting schemes and sensitivity of results is undertaken in Chapter 5. Data sources are discussed more fully in Chapters 5 and 6 and in Appendix A. The non-US bloc is defined as the other G7 members. By implication, there is a 'rest-of-the-world' that is not modelled and considered as exogenous.
5. These conclusions are again not dependent on the type of interest rate, or the method of deriving real rates. See, for example, the work of Blanchard and Summers (1984).
6. The current account numbers do not exactly reflect capital flows when central

banks intervene in the foreign exchange markets. At least until 1987, sustained foreign exchange intervention has not been a major feature of the floating-rate period.

7. There are, however, some economists who believe that freely operating financial markets may become unstable and driven by speculative bubbles. See, as an example, Krugman (1986).

8. The three shocks include the two increases in oil prices in 1974–5 and 1979, as well as the fall in oil prices in 1985–6.

9. The United Kingdom is the main exception to this statement. Its debt outstanding has been stable, although at high levels, over the period.

Part I
Theoretical Issues

Chapter 2

Intertemporal models

Introduction

During the 1960s and early 1970s the intertemporal implications of fiscal policy were largely neglected. Keynesian approaches to anti-cyclical macro-policy issues were popular both at the academic and the applied level. Fiscal policies were implemented without any permanent rise in debt-to-GNP ratios in most of the industrial countries. Budget deficits were allowed to expand during recessions, but were reduced during periods of recovery. As was seen in Chapter 1, the role and importance of deficit financing in fiscal programmes has changed substantially since the mid- to late 1970s. Almost all industrial countries have used permanent rises in debt levels to finance ongoing expenditure increases and/or tax cuts. The ongoing use of debt financing, long after any anti-cyclical justification for deficits has passed, is in sharp contrast to the previous Keynesian policy approaches of the 1960s. The case of the United States has attracted most attention, as there is no sign of the US fiscal imbalance being addressed in the near future.

The impact effect of this expansion in public sector debt is easy to see; it has, for example, enabled the US government to cut taxes, while at the same time increasing certain areas of public spending. What is not so obvious (at least to some) is that the rise in debt outstanding has important implications for the future. The debt stock cannot continue indefinitely to outpace the growth in gross national product and has major implications for future tax and/or expenditure policies.

Given these substantial changes in the very nature of fiscal policy that have occurred since the mid- to late 1970s, it is not surprising that macroeconomists have again turned their attention to the intertemporal aspects that are inherent in the alternative methods of financing government spending. The aim of this chapter is to review these intertemporal issues — issues that are the core of the empirical work undertaken in Part II of the book. While it is true that most of the empirical models tested in this area are not derived themselves from intertemporal optimization problems, they invariably are testing dynamic intertemporal hypotheses. It is therefore necessary to understand where these hypotheses come from.

Discussion of the effects of public debt in an intertemporal setting to go back as far as Ricardo and the issue has been a controversial one ever since governments have been in debt. The review undertaken here is not designed to cover all writings on the subject, but to present some standard and accepted conclusions that come out of the intertemporal literature.[1] The major issue that flows through all of this literature is whether changes in the level of government debt will have real effects on the economy as a whole.

The chapter is structured as follows. It first addresses the debt neutrality issue. This is most easily discussed in the closed economy framework. The major contributions of the literature is to show that, under certain conditions, changes in the level of public debt will indeed be neutral. Much of the theoretical work is related to showing just how important the restrictions are for debt neutrality to hold and what happens if they do not hold.

The chapter then goes on to look at the recent attempts to extend the theoretical intertemporal models to the open economy framework. These models have not, as yet, been used extensively in the empirical field, so the aim will be briefly to set out the conclusions from this work rather than to derive all the possible results that they produce. The emphasis is placed on highlighting those conclusions that are different to the standard income-expenditure models (reviewed in Chapter 3). After briefly stating how debt neutrality works in the open economy, the bulk of this part of the chapter is devoted to looking at intertemporal models which allow for deviations from the extreme Ricardian case. The chapter closes by summarizing the important hypotheses that are obtained from the intertemporal literature.

The primary conclusions drawn from this chapter include the following. First, the Ricardian Equivalence Theorem is a real theoretical possibility that requires empirical testing. Second, it is likely that tests of Ricardian equivalence will be more powerful if they include debt levels rather than only deficits. Third, tests of Ricardian equivalence should allow for open economy considerations. Finally, there are much clearer and less ambiguous effects of debt on interest rates than on exchange rates in a non-neutral world.

The closed economy

This section is devoted to examining the implications of government debt in the closed economy. It starts with a brief review of the concepts of intertemporal accounting, emphasizing, in particular, the importance of the government's own budget constraints. It then moves on to derive formally the possibility of debt neutrality in the simplest possible model and spells out the restrictions that are necessary to ensure the neutrality result. Finally, it outlines the implications for financial markets when these restrictions do not hold.

Intertemporal constraints

In the standard IS/LM models of the economy, the government faces a temporal financial constraint (even this is not always explicit). All government expenditure must be financed by taxes, by printing money or by borrowing from the public.[2] This can be written (excluding money financing) as

$$\bar{g}_t + r_t b_t = \tau_t + \dot{b}_t \tag{2.1}$$

All notation used in the chapter is provided in Table 2.1. The first point to note from equation (2.1) is that the temporal constraint does not appear to be much of a constraint on government spending at all. It states that the government can spend as much as it likes for any given level of taxes, it merely involves expanding the deficit.[3]

The real constraint on the government's ability to spend is an intertemporal one. It is already apparent in equation (2.1). If, for example, the government decides to cut taxes at time t then, in the following period, the amount of bonds outstanding will be higher; interest payments will also be higher. If the government wishes to maintain its spending and tax

Table 2.1 List of notation

c	=	private consumption
y	=	real output
$\bar{y}_d$	=	lifetime disposable income
w	=	real wealth
r	=	real interest rate
τ	=	real taxes
m	=	real money
b	=	real bonds
g	=	government spending (including interest payments)
$\bar{g}$	=	government spending on goods and services
ϱ	=	life expectancy parameter
δ	=	subjective discount factor
α	=	international present-value factor
U	=	private sector utility

Note: A dot over a variable represents a time derivative. The subscript t is used throughout the book to indicate time.

policies unchanged in period $t + 1$, the deficit will be even higher, as will the level of debt in period $t + 2$. This cannot be continued indefinitely and the government will eventually have to raise taxes (and to a level higher than at time t) to prevent interest payments from going to infinity.[4] The simple point is that any debt financing introduced in the current period will always have implications for future fiscal decisions.

This point is seen most clearly by writing out the government's intertemporal budget constraint. To keep the example simple, assume that the government lives for two periods.[5] It can issue bonds in the first period, but must pay them back in the second (with interest). Then

$$\bar{g}_t + \alpha\bar{g}_{t+1} + \alpha(1 + r_t)b_{t+1} = \tau_t + \alpha\tau_{t+1} + b_t \qquad (2.2)$$

where $\alpha = (1 + r_t)^{-1}$. The left hand side of equation (2.2) is the government's lifetime expenditures. It consists of spending on goods and services in the first and second periods, as well as interest payments on any first-period borrowing and the repayment of that borrowing in the second period. The right hand side represents the government's receipts. It comprises first- and second-period taxes, along with any first-period borrowing receipts.

Two important points can be drawn from the intertemporal constraint. First, it is clear that debt cancels out on both sides of equation, that is, the government cannot derive any windfall gains by borrowing in the current period (or any period). Second, an expansionary deficit policy in the first period will always be followed by an even larger contractionary policy in the second period. This results because of the need to pay interest on the debt incurred to finance the initial expansion. As a more concrete example, if the US government were able to achieve its target of balancing the budget by 1991, it would imply — given the higher level of US debt outstanding and assuming no changes to non-interest spending levels — that the initial tax cuts of the early 1980s would not only need to be reversed, but taxes would have to be raised by an additional $100 billion a year, just to cover the interest costs.[6]

It is this intertemporal constraint on the government that is the key feature of models that produce debt neutrality; the next section sets out why and when this is likely to happen.

Debt neutrality

The Richard Equivalence Theorem claims that for a given level of government spending on goods and services, any switch between bond and tax financing will have no real effects. In particular, it implies there will be no impact on real interest and exchange rates from a budget deficit generated by cutting taxes; a sharp contrast to the standard IS/LM results. The reason for the debt-neutrality result is very simple and has already been alluded to. In the static IS/LM model a tax cut puts upward pressure on interest rates by inducing individuals to spend and by inducing them to demand higher real money balances. Both of these effects occur because the rise in the bond stock makes people feel wealthier. If, however, people recognize that a tax cut now implies a rise in future taxes to repay bondholders, that is, if they understand the implications of the government's intertemporal budget constraint, then the future tax liabilities will be incorporated into their present-value wealth estimate, offsetting exactly the windfall they receive from the current tax cut. With no increase in perceived wealth, there can be no rise in private spending or money demand — the interest rate and the exchange rate are therefore unaffected.

This can be derived formally in the simple two-period intertemporal optimization framework, where individuals maximize consumption over a two period lifespan. The utility function is of the form

$$U = U(c_t, c_{t+1}). \tag{2.3}$$

Individuals maximize subject to their intertemporal budget constraint:

$$c_t + \alpha c_{t+1} = y_t - \tau_t + \alpha(y_{t+1} - \tau_{t+1}) \equiv \bar{y}_d. \tag{2.4}$$

Equation (2.4) says that the present value of lifetime consumption is equated to the present value of lifetime disposable income. Solving the optimization problem posed in (2.3) and (2.4) gives the conventional Fisherian consumption function:

$$c_t = C(r_t, \bar{y}_d). \tag{2.5}$$

It would appear at first glance that by reducing current taxes the government could indeed raise the individual's lifetime income and consumption. However, that can only happen by ignoring the government's own intertemporal budget constraint.

For convenience, it is possible to rewrite the government's budget constraint (already derived in equation (2.2)) without the bond stocks as

$$\bar{g}_t + \alpha \bar{g}_{t+1} = \tau_t + \alpha \tau_{t+1}. \tag{2.6}$$

Equation (2.6) makes it clear that the present value of government spending must equal the present value of taxes. As both period taxes enter into the definition of private lifetime disposable income, it is possible to substitute out taxes from the private sector's disposable income, resulting in the following consumption function,

$$c_t = C(r_t, (y_t - \bar{g}_t) + \alpha(y_{t+1} - \bar{g}_{t+1})). \qquad (2.7)$$

It follows from equation (2.7) that changes to the tax/bond mix can have no impact on private sector activity because it is only government spending that enters the private sector's optimization problem.[7]

There are a number of key assumptions required in the derivation of the Ricardian results that have been attacked by subsequent writers. First, the assumption that the interest rates used to discount future changes to the individual's and government's budget constraints are the same is implausible. If, as seems likely, the government can access the financial markets at a cheaper rate than the individual, a tax-cut-induced deficit will provide the individual with a means of shifting consumption intertemporally at a lower intertemporal price.[8] A second assumption is that taxes are non-distortionary. If the imposition of taxes distorts private sector behaviour, then a tax cut may affect consumption decisions and financial markets.[9]

An even more fundamental criticism is that individuals and governments generally have different time horizons when forming their budget constraints. This was formally presented in the model of Diamond (1965). He introduced the overlapping generations model to the fiscal literature. The implications of this can be seen by adjusting the individual's budget constraint (equation (2.4)) to allow for the possibility of overlapping generations and retirement in the second period. The individual's budget constraint now simplifies to

$$c_t + \alpha c_{t+1} = y_t - \tau_t \equiv \bar{y}_d. \qquad (2.8)$$

In this case, lifetime disposable income is a function of the government's tax and debt policy, even though the government continues to be bound by the two-period budget constraint. This occurs because the people who gain from a fiscal expansion will not be obliged to pay the higher second-period taxes. Government debt allows the current generation to shift the burden of lower taxes now to the next generation who will pay higher taxes.

The overlapping-generation, finite-life model did not put an end to the Ricardian Equivalence Theorem. Barro (1974) has shown, by allowing for bequests and adding the utility of the individual's offspring to his own utility function, the traditional neutrality still goes through. The result is intuitively simple. If your utility is affected by the fact that your offspring will have to pay the taxes you avoid, then you will ensure (via a bequest), your offspring's disposable income is not affected by fiscal policy. The Barro assumptions mean that even an individual with a finite life will feel the effects of future taxation and will react by saving more now, removing any upward pressure on interest rates that would otherwise develop.

A final assumption that may not be realistic in the derivation of debt neutrality is the requirement that debt be fully repaid in the two-period model (or that the outstanding debt stock approaches some terminal level in the infinite horizon model). Such an assumption seems highly unlikely in reality as there are many reasons why the level of debt may be changed permanently, without breaking the government's intertemporal budget constraint.[10] As shown in Carmichael (1984), once this possibility is allowed for, the neutrality results no longer hold. In particular, changes to the level of government debt substitute one for one with the private sector's demand for other financial instruments, including claims to real capital. The reduced demand for other assets will have direct effects on financial markets, by lowering asset prices and raising the rate of return on these assets. The reason for this is that individuals decide upon the size of their optimal portfolio of financial assets based on their need to transfer consumption intertemporally. If the government exogenously increases the amount of financial instruments available for savings purposes, then individuals will not increase their total demand for financial instruments, but will substitute the government bonds into their existing portfolio. This can only be done by reducing the value of other outstanding financial instruments; in turn, raising the overall yields on those instruments. According to Carmichael's model, this channel is likely to exert a much stronger and more permanent affect on financial markets than the standard consumption function channel.

To conclude, the debt-neutrality theorem is the logical outcome of rational forward-looking individuals recognizing the fact that the government cannot finance its spending without taking away real resources from the private sector. Once the private sector has decided on its optimal intertemporal consumption path, the government is not able to alter that path by adjusting the path of the private sectors disposable income. However, the question of how relevant the Ricardian conclusions are to the real world is another issue altogether, one that is dependent on a whole range of restrictive assumptions which can only be tested empirically.

Financial market implications

Before moving on to the open economy literature, it is worth examining, in more detail, the financial market implications of the theoretical models outlined above. Unfortunately, the majority of the intertemporal models developed to date do not have very detailed financial market sectors. This is not surprising given the early development stage of this approach and the difficulties of introducing financial assets into a microeconomic decision-making process. At the same time, a number of simple and strong conclusions can be drawn from them. First, in a model where consumers are infinitely lived, or have infinite horizons via the bequest motive; where there are no imperfections in financial markets; where taxes are non-distortionary;[11] where all assets are perfect substitutes; and where terminal conditions are placed on government borrowing, then the issue of public sector debt to replace tax financing will have no impact on financial markets. This hypothesis, known as the Ricardian Equivalence Theorem, is very straightforward and should be easily tested. Other interesting issues can also be addressed within Ricardian type models. They are particularly suited to analysing welfare issues, as they provide a bench-mark — the Ricardian solution — against which policy-making and market imperfections can be evaluated. These normative issues will not be pursued in this book. The emphasis throughout will be put on the question of whether debt neutrality does or does not hold. If debt neutrality does not hold, the next question is to determine what are the expected results for financial markets.

In the early models, such as Diamond's, the relaxation of the Ricardian assumptions implies that a tax cut financed by borrowing will stimulate private consumption. This leads indirectly to higher real interest rates via the goods markets; that is, the interest rate must rise to equilibrate the savings investment imbalance. Moreover, in the context of a model that contains capital (as in the Diamond model), the rise in the current period's interest rate will lower the next periods capital stock and further undermines the future generation's welfare.[12] The final equilibrium indicates that individuals have rearranged their portfolios by incorporating the higher level of government debt, at the expense of the capital stock. The causal mechanism is via higher consumption and interest rates. Consumption does not rise in the steady state because of the lower capital stock.

More recently, these same conclusions have been reproduced by Blanchard (1985). He uses a more sophisticated version of the Diamond model where consumers have uncertain life horizons, while the government's is infinite. Specifically, in the world of Blanchard, all individuals face a fixed probability of death (ϱ). This fixed probability of dying raises the individual's cost of borrowing above the market rate at which the government can borrow, thus breaking the key Ricardian assumption that all agents can access world financial markets at the same cost. He comes to the same overall conclusions as Diamond: an increase in debt raises consumption on impact, increasing interest rates and lowering capital accumulation. In the long-run, both consumption and capital are lower, but interest rates remain higher. Although Blanchard's own results do not provide any major new insights into debt and deficits, his methodology has proved to be useful in attacking the more complex open economy issues.

The above results, while being intuitively appealing, are achieved without any realistic financial market disaggregation. Portfolio preferences are not introduced by assuming all assets are perfect substitutes. Money is generally omitted from the analysis. Nevertheless, the models do at least provide some clear-cut hypotheses that are the alternatives to the Ricardian hypothesis; that is if the Ricardian assumptions do not hold, then we expect, following a (tax-cut-induced) debt expansion, interest rates to rise, consumption to rise (at least in the short run), and the capital stock to fall.

Open economy extensions

The open economy extensions of the intertemporal optimization approach have followed three directions: one using the infinite horizon neutrality framework as in Stockman (1980; 1983), Lucas (1982) and Frenkel and Razin (1985); one directly applying the Diamond model to the open economy as in Buiter (1981), Persson (1985) and Van Wijnbergen (1986a); and finally, one strand of the literature has used the model as developed by Blanchard (1985), as in Frenkel and Razin (1986a; 1986b; 1986c).[13] This section reviews briefly each of these groups, with the most attention placed on the second and third, which give debt policy some real role in the open economy.

Infinite horizon models

The finite horizon optimization model has been used in a variety of open economy situations. In the models of Stockman (1980; 1983) and Lucas (1982), monetory issues are examined in general equilibrium specifications. Obstfeld (1981) and Dornbusch (1983) look at the welfare implications of asset stock adjustment in the open economy. None of these works discuss fiscal issues in any detail so are not reviewed here. More recently, however, Frenkel and Razin (1985) have used this framework to examine the role of government spending in the determination of interest rates and exchange rates. In all of these models the infinite horizon of consumers ensures that Ricardian equivalence holds. They do not provide any role for public sector deficits. It is worth, however, looking at the effects of fiscal spending in these models, so that the direct expenditure effects of deficits in intertemporal models can be compared with the Mundell–Fleming results for a balanced budget expansion.

For this purpose it is useful to examine the model of Frenkel and Razin (1985). The model builds upon the intertemporal maximization problem,

$$U = \sum_{t=0}^{\infty} \delta^t \log c_t, \tag{2.9}$$

where δ is specified as the subjective discount factor which may differ from the world rate of interest. The private sector's budget constraint is

$$\sum_{t=0}^{\infty} \alpha_t c_t = \sum_{t=0}^{\infty} \alpha_t y_t - \sum_{t=0}^{\infty} \alpha_t \tau_t - b \equiv \bar{y}_d, \tag{2.10}$$

where α is the present-value factor, in this case the inverse of all relevant future interest rates. These equations are just the two-period equations (2.3) and (2.4) extended to the infinite horizon, with an initial debt stock, b, included. The budget constraint for the government is

$$\sum_{t=0}^{\infty} \alpha_t g_t = \sum_{t=0}^{\infty} \alpha_t \tau_t. \tag{2.11}$$

This budget constraint ensures that the present value of government spending equals the present value of future taxes (as in equation (2.6)). The time path of public debt is again irrelevant to the private sector. The solution for private consumption is

$$c_t = (1 - \delta)\omega_t, \tag{2.12}$$

where $\omega_t = (\delta_t/\alpha_t)\bar{y}_d$. This is the same as in the previous two-period Ricardian example, except that consumption is also now affected by the external rate of interest that can differ from the home rate of time preference. The second important difference between this and the previous Ricardian example is that equilibrium is obtained (and the interest rate determined) by the condition that world output equals world consumption.

In this two-country world, the effect of government spending on the world interest rate works through the individual's budget constraint by reducing disposable income and wealth. However, because the marginal propensity to consume out of wealth is less than unity, the reduction in wealth will be associated with an excess demand for goods which is satisfied by a trade deficit and higher external borrowing on impact. The rise in the home country's external debt also means a rise in the foreign country's wealth, reinforcing the excess demand for goods and inducing a rise in the world rate of interest. The rise in the rate of interest crowds out spending at home and abroad. In the steady state, the interest rate will be higher (lower) depending on whether the foreign country's propensity to save out of its higher level of wealth is lower (higher) than that of the home country.

The above model was also extended to incorporate a terms-of-trade or real exchange rate by introducing home and foreign goods separately into the utility function of each country. The detailed results become somewhat involved in this case, but one clear point does emerge from the analysis: a key determinant of the exchange-rate response to a rise in government spending is the relative propensities of the government and the private sector to spend on foreign goods. If, as is often assumed, governments tend to spend more on home goods, then a rise in government spending will tend to raise the price of home goods, that is appreciate the exchange rate. As will be seen in Chapter 3, this is a result common to many models.

Finite horizon models

The finite horizon models can be split into two groups: one that follows the Diamond overlapping-generations framework; and one that uses the uncertain lifetime framework of Blanchard. As for the closed economy, both approaches produce similar qualitative conclusions that government debt issue will be important for the behaviour of financial markets.

One of the first attempts to look at the open economy implications of public debt was by Persson (1985). Persson's model first extends the Diamond approach to the case of the small open economy. His model is very simple, with only one good and a single world rate of interest. Issues of exchange-rate dynamics are therefore not relevant. With the domestic rate of interest now tied to the world rate, a deficit is financed by external borrowing and there is no crowding-out of investment. The results are in stark contrast to the closed economy. There is no impact crowding-out via higher interest rates, nor is there a reduction in the capital stock. The trade account goes into deficit because of higher domestic consumption out of the higher wealth, which, in turn, runs down net foreign assets. In the steady state, taxes must rise to pay the higher interest burden and so consumption falls. Here then, is the first (of many) examples that show that the closed and open economy implications of higher public debt can be very different. The important point is that the use of a small open economy to test for the effects of debt on interest rates is not going to be a relevant test of Ricardian equivalence.

Persson also examines a two-country version of the Diamond model. The results for a fiscal expansion are, not surprisingly, a combination of the close and small open economy models: interest rates rise, but by less than the closed economy example; the current account goes into deficit, but by less than in the small open economy example. The limitations of the Persson model relate mainly to the degree of simplification, and particularly the lack of a real exchange rate and exchange-rate expectations.

This makes any comparisons with the Mundell–Fleming results discussed in Chapter 3 rather hazardous.

Using the same framework Van Wijnbergen (1986a) has extended the Diamond model even further by using a two-good, two-country analysis, making the results much more consistent with traditional macro-models. The introduction of two goods does not greatly alter the general interest-rate response; the deficit triggers a rise in home consumption of both goods, putting upward pressure on the world interest rate. The exchange-rate response is ambiguous, again (as for the spending shock discussed above) depending on the relative consumption propensities. If the home country consumes relatively more than foreigners of its own good, then the domestic currency will appreciate. If spending patterns across countries are the same, there will be no impact on relative goods prices.

Paralleling the development of the two period Diamond-type models has been the extension of the uncertain lifetime model to the open economy. The original Blanchard (1985) article, in fact, included cases for the small open economy. His open economy model was similar to the simple one-good, single-interest-rate model used by Persson. Not surprisingly, the two models provide almost identical conclusions and need no further discussion. The approach has since been taken up by Frenkel and Razin (1986a; 1986b) to give their, originally infinite-horizon, fiscal policy model more generality.

Adding the possibility of an uncertain life horizon to the Frenkel and Razin model produces a consumption function that is dependent on the fixed probability of death:

$$c_t = (1 - \varrho\delta)\omega_t. \tag{2.13}$$

All other aspects of the two-country model remain unchanged. The impact effect of a budget deficit (resulting from a tax cut) now raises the current generation's wealth; that generation will now be expecting to repay only a fraction (determined by ϱ) of the higher future taxes. The initial effects are very similar to those derived by Persson (1985): higher wealth at home generates higher consumption and lower savings; the rate of interest must rise on impact. The rise in the rate of interest lowers foreign wealth and spending so that the home current account goes unambiguously into deficit. The steady-state effects of the higher government debt outstanding must also be a higher steady-state rate of interest. This is not because lower taxes can raise wealth in the steady state, but because lower taxes in the current period imply higher taxes in the steady state. A higher long-run of interest is therefore required to induce an increase in savings and prevent a fall in steady-state wealth.[14]

Frenkel and Razin (1986b) extend the Blanchard version of their model to allow for the presence of non-traded goods. The inclusion of more than one good again makes the maths difficult to see through, but the results are intuitively straightforward and similar to other models containing more than one good. The deficit again raises current home spending (via the same wealth channels as above) and lowers foreign spending (because of its impact on interest rates); given the assumptions of the model,[15] the price of non-traded goods will rise at home and fall abroad. To quote Frankel and Razin (1986b, p. 106):

> since the budget deficit transfers income from future generations (whose propensity to spend on present goods is zero) to the current generation (whose propensity to spend on present goods is positive), it creates an excess demand for present tradable goods resulting in a rise in their intertemporal relative price (the rate of interest). Likewise, it creates an excess demand for domestic non-tradable goods and an excess supply of foreign non-tradable goods and changes the temporal relative prices (the real exchange rates).

Testable hypotheses

Before moving on to models that are not derived from intertemporal problems, it is now worth summarizing some of the important testable hypotheses that have been raised in the theoretical work reviewed so far. The first point is that the hypotheses are very different depending on whether closed or open economy assumptions are employed. If one is prepared to use closed economy models, then the testable hypotheses are relatively straightforward:

1 An increase in the current debt/tax mix will lead to higher interest rates only if the private sector does not discount the additional future taxes. If the private sector does fully discount future taxes then debt policy will have no influence on interest rates.
2 If individuals do not expect to have to repay the debt, they will substitute debt in their portfolios for other financial assets, such as capital.

In the framework of the open economy, the issues are much more complex. The response of the real interest rate to fiscal shocks is now determined jointly with the real exchange rate and depends very much on the exact model specification. However, a number of simple hypotheses do stand out:

1 For a small open economy, the effect of deficits will show up as a short-run rise in consumption and a current account deficit.

2 For a small open economy, the permanent effect of a rise in public debt is a long-run fall in net foreign assets.
3 In a two-country model, a rise in public debt should affect both interest rates and exchange rates. However, the size and direction of the changes are dependent on model parameters.

As already mentioned, one of the main weaknesses of the intertemporal approach is the lack of financial structure. This is particularly apparent in the open economy versions where arbitrage linkages between interest and exchange rates are usually ignored. Without such linkages it is difficult to make very confident statements about financial markets and this is one of the main reasons why intertemporal models have not received much attention from empirical economists, at least at the international level. The following chapter deals with the traditional income-expenditure models of fiscal policy, where financial markets are developed to a much greater degree.

Notes

1. Some of the early writings include Buchanan (1958), Modigliani (1961), and Diamond (1965) to mention just a few. Modigliani (1961) contains a good summary of the traditional debates on the dynamic effects of government debt.
2. Throughout the book the emphasis will be put on real economic variables. Monetary financing of deficits will not be discussed. This does not seem to be a dramatic simplification given that seigniorage has historically played only a small role in financing deficits in the industrial countries (see Buiter 1985). For a more detailed discussion of the monetary aspects of the government budget constraint see Sargent and Wallace (1982) and Van Wijnbergen (1985).
3. The budget constraint above is about the simplest one that can be discussed to highlight issues of debt neutrality. The actual budget constraint facing a government is much more complex and depends, to a large extent, on the definition of the public sector. See Buiter (1983) for a more complete description of the government budget constraint. Throughout the book the government is defined as the central government and excludes public sector corporations, unless otherwise stated. This definition is adopted not on theoretical grounds but because of data availability.
4. The analysis in this chapter does not include the case of the growing economy. As is discussed in Diamond (1965) and more recently in Cohen (1985), it is possible for the government to borrow to finance future debt servicing if the rate of growth of the economy exceeds the rate of interest.
5. The same basic conclusions can be drawn if the government is infinitely lived, so long as a terminal constraint is placed on government debt.
6. This is, of course, a ballpark figure that depends very much on the level of interest rates. It is a very conservative guesstimate based on the likely increase in US debt between 1980 and 1991 of around $2 trillion along with a nominal interest rate of around 5 per cent.
7. This simple derivation of the Ricardian Equivalence Theorem is based largely on Mutoh (1985).

8. A very recent study of this possibility by Yotsuzuka (1987), has thrown some doubt on the generality of this argument. Using informationally imperfect capital markets, he shows that the Ricardian results may still go through.
9. See Barro (1974).
10. See Barro (1979) for a discussion of this question.
11. Throughout this chapter we analyse the case of non-distortionary taxes. The effects of distortionary taxes are analysed by Barro (1974), Aschauer and Greenwood (1985) and Frenkel and Razin (1987).
12. The welfare implications actually depend on whether the economy was initially above or below the 'golden rule' growth path in the Diamond model.
13. Frenkel and Razin (1987) is a useful reference that discusses nearly all aspects of this intertemporal literature in an international setting.
14. The steady-state results seem to be highly dependent on the terminal conditions imposed on debt. In this non-Ricardian version, Frenkel and Razin do not impose a zero terminal condition on debt, so that the one-period deficit raises the level of debt permanently; hence the higher steady-state interest burden. Although not discussed in their model, there are two important intertemporal aspects of non-neutrality: one is related to the flow effects of deficits and future taxes associated with servicing higher debt; the other to the permanent stock effects of public sector debt that can be used as a substitute for other methods of intertemporal substitution.
15. See Frenkel and Razin (1986c), where it is shown that nearly all of the interest- and exchange-rate results from the intertemporal models are dependent on more detailed parameter specification, especially the relative intertemporal consumption propensities across countries and across sectors.

Chapter 3

The non-Ricardian world

Introduction

The previous chapter outlined the conditions under which debt neutrality would hold. One of these conditions was that consumption decisions must be made by consumers who optimize intertemporally. However, in traditional macroeconomic models, consumption and savings decisions are based only on current variables, ensuring that shifts between tax and debt financing do have real effects. Although the traditional income-expenditure models are open to criticism of being *ad hoc*, they do have the advantage of providing more insight into complex temporal substitution issues; particularly in the area of financial markets. Moreover, while not derived from micro-foundations, these models can provide insights into intertemporal issues using long-run and dynamic multipliers. This chapter will review the basic results of the income-expenditure model, with the aim of coming up with a set of testable hypotheses that will either correspond, or provide alternatives to, the hypotheses outlined in the previous chapter.

One of the central themes of the analysis (which also follows the previous chapter) is the importance of international linkages for the crowding-out hypothesis. While the theoretical literature has long recognized the importance of the open economy, closed economy assumptions are often still applied in empirical work. By concentrating on the open-economy framework, the chapter stresses that interest-rate and exchange-rate responses to fiscal policy are determined simultaneously and depend upon the structural characteristics of the open economy, that is, capital mobility, asset substitutability, expectations formation, and so on.

A second important theme is the need to distinguish between deficits generated by tax cuts and through spending increases. This aspect is generally not emphasized in traditional macroeconomics, but was seen in Chapter 3 to be of vital importance in any empirical analysis of the Ricardian Equivalence Theorem. Unfortunately, many model-builders do not discuss the tax/debt swap policy separately from deficit-financed spending shocks. For the purposes of the analysis here, it will be necessary to concentrate mostly on the effects of higher government debt. To do this, it is useful to keep separate the expenditure-inducing or transactions effects of deficits from the portfolio and wealth effects of public debt.

A third issue that is stressed throughout the chapter is the need to look at both the short- and long-run effects of budget deficits. In particular, the conventional Mundell–Fleming model treats expectations, asset stocks and prices as fixed over the horizon under analysis. Once more realistic dynamics are allowed for, the traditional results are sometimes modified substantially. This does not, however, imply that there is no role for short-run comparative statics. Rather, such analysis should be accompanied by at least some discussion of the medium- and longer-term effects of running budget deficits. In moving to the world of long-term full equilibrium, the issues change from questions of stabilization, to questions about sustainability of deficits, stability, and optimal debt levels. These medium-term issues are, in fact, often more important than the issues of short-term stabilization, and are crucial to the question of international economic policy management.

It should be stressed at the outset that the approach taken is to concentrate on macro-policy. Doing so ignores much of the finance literature on the determination of the term structure of interest rates and many microeconomic issues associated with the effects of fiscal actions on financial markets. Similarly, the huge literature on monetary models of exchange rates is given little attention, as it provides only a limited role for the analysis of fiscal policy.

The chapter is organized as follows. The following section starts with a review of the static closed economy model. The central section of the chapter looks at the open economy implications of fiscal policy. It is subdivided into three parts. The first presents the simplest static results from the Mundell–Fleming model with fixed prices. Extending the Mundell–Fleming model to include flexible prices and wealth effects is shown to enrich the analysis but leave most of the fundamental results intact. The second examines more recent versions of the Mundell–Fleming model that incorporate the dynamic effects of asset stock adjustment and expectations. The third goes a step further by introducing imperfect asset substitutability. The chapter is concluded with a comparison of the results obtained from Chapters 2 and 3, the aim being to highlight key hypotheses that require empirical exploration.

The closed economy model

The aim of this section is to set out the effects of debt/tax swap policy in the closed economy. This is done using a very simple income-expenditure model.

The original and subsequent textbook versions of the income-expenditure model were used primarily to address issues of stabilization policy. The time horizon was the short run, enabling the use of such simplifying assumptions as fixed prices and expectations, exogenous asset stocks and zero wealth effects. For this review, one of the most important implications of these assumptions is that the interest rates and exchange rates discussed are real rates and are not distinguished from nominal rates. Such an approach, while perhaps acceptable in the fixed exchange-rate, stable inflation environment of the 1950s and 1960s, became increasingly unrealistic during the 1970s and it will be important to extend the model to allow for these complications. However, a number of key issues can be most clearly highlighted within the simplest model, and certain fundamental conclusions are not altered by complex extensions.

The simplest income-extenditure model contains an IS curve or goods market,

$$y = c(y - \tau) + i(r) + g, \tag{3.1}$$

where $0 < c_y < 1$ and $i_r < 0$, and a money market,

$$M/P = M(y,r), \tag{3.2}$$

where $M_y > 0$ and $M_r < 0$. All notation used in this chapter is listed in Table 3.1. The parenthesis indicate a functional relationship so that $M(y,r)$ implies money demand (M) is a function of both income (y) and the interest rate (r). For notational ease the partial derivatives are expressed with a subscript; that is, M_r denotes the response of money demand to a change in the interest rate.

The restrictions on the partial derivatives are standard and require little explanation. The IS curve (equation (3.1)) and can be solved with the LM curve (equation (3.2)) for income and the interest rate. Solving the above system for changes in government spending and taxes yields the standard Keynesian results that expansionary fiscal policy puts upward pressure on interest rates. For an increase in government spending the interest response is given by

$$\frac{dr}{dg} = -\frac{M_y}{M_r(1 - c_y) + i_r M_y} > 0, \tag{3.3}$$

and for a fall in taxes by

$$\frac{dr}{-dr} = c_y \frac{dr}{dg} > 0 \tag{3.4}$$

Table 3.1 List of notation

c	=	private consumption
i	=	private investment
y	=	real output
y_d	=	disposable income
w	=	real wealth
r	=	real interest rate
e	=	real exchange rate (a rise in e represents a depreciation)
τ	=	real taxes
nfa	=	net foreign asset position
ca	=	current account
m	=	real money
b	=	real bonds
$\bar{g}$	=	government spending on goods and services
tb	=	trade balance (in domestic currency)
x	=	home country's export good
im	=	home country's import (foreign country's export) good
E	=	forward expectations operator

Notes: Capital letters refer to nominal variables and lower case letters refer to real variables. A dot over a variable represents a time derivative. An asterisk denotes a foreign country variable.

Despite the extreme simplicity of the model, it is already able to show that there is a difference between deficits that result from fiscal spending and deficits that result from tax cuts. The factor which dampens the effect of taxes on interest rates is the marginal propensity to spend out of disposable income c_y. When this is close to unity as is generally assumed in Keynesian models, both fiscal multipliers are similar and there may be little need to distinguish between the two. However, if one takes a life-cycle view of consumption, that is, the intertemporal view that was presented in Chapter 3 (and people believe the tax cut will not be permanent), then the impact on disposable income may be very small. A deficit associated with a tax cut will then have little or no impact on private expenditure and therefore on interest rates. However, even in this case, a deficit which is caused by a rise in spending will still lead to an increase in interest rates. As in the previous intertemporal models, the fundamental assumptions determining the size of the expenditure effects of tax/debt policy relative to spending policy are the horizon of the policy action (whether it will be reversed), and second, whether the private sector incorporates this fact into the calculation of disposable income.

The size of the interest-rate response also depends on all the parameters of the model, but the income elasticity of money is particularly important. If M_y is close to zero, then there will be no effect on interest rates. This would imply a flat LM curve, something that is generally not supported by the empirical evidence. Indeed, one of the main debates of the 1960s between the Keynesian and monetarist groups was whether the LM curve was vertical. Both groups recognized that fiscal spending put upward pressure on interest rates, although the relative importance of this was hotly contested (see Friedman 1972).

In the analysis so far, the effects of fiscal deficits on interest rates have worked through expenditure channels. This reflects the fact that the income-expenditure model is built using a flow definition of equilibrium, rather than a stock approach. The model ignores the fact that financing the deficit requires adding to the stock of outstanding debt that is held within the private sector's portfolio of assets. To capture this portfolio channel in the model it is necessary to add financial wealth as an argument in the money demand function. For consistency it is also useful to include a wealth effect in the private sector's consumption function, where wealth is defined as

$$w = m + b.$$

Assume that the marginal propensity to spend out of wealth is positive ($c_w > 0$) and that wealth also enters the money demand function with a positive sign ($m_w > 0$). Then, for the case with wealth effects, the solution for a fiscal expansion is

$$\frac{dr}{db} = -\frac{(1 - c_y)m_w + m_y(1 + c_w)}{m_r(1 - c_y) + i_r m_y} > 0. \tag{3.5}$$

The result is not only unambiguously positive, it is also larger than the traditional impact effect examined above. The rise in wealth associated with the rise in the bond stock leads directly to higher interest rates via an increased demand for money, and indirectly via the effects of higher wealth on consumption. The solution for a bond-financed tax cut is similar, but again reduced by the marginal propensity to consume. In the case with wealth effects, however, even if consumers use a life-cycle type consumption function and expect to pay higher taxes in the future, there will still be a rise in interest rates because of the permanent rise in debt generated by a one-period deficit. Debt-financed fiscal policy shifts both the IS and LM curves in this model; and with both curves shifting up, there must always be a rise in the rate of interest.

There is one further extension which is generally little discussed in standard textbook models, but which does modify the above results. This is the inclusion of additional assets within the private sector's portfolio. Friedman (1978) has shown that the inclusion of real capital in the IS/LM model leads to the possibility that the portfolio effects of budget deficits dominate the flow effects from higher spending, leading to a lower real rate of return on capital. This can occur when money and bonds are closer substitutes to each other than bonds and real capital. Because of problems of tractability, the analysis of the dynamics of real capital accumulation is generally ignored in the open economy literature. In conformity with the literature, the assumption of perfect substitutability between capital and bonds will be adopted through the rest of the chapter. It should be kept in mind, however, that the exact characteristics of the bonds issued to finance deficits are very important for determining the response of financial markets to changes in the financing strategies of the government.[1]

The open economy

This section takes the simple model set out above and extends it (one step at a time) to incorporate the most recent theoretical advances in open economy macroeconomics. Throughout, it will be assumed that debt neutrality does not hold.

The static Mundell–Fleming model

The Mundell–Fleming model extends the IS/LM framework by including a trade balance function in the goods market:

$$y = c(y - \tau) + i(r) + g + tb(y, y^\star, e), \tag{3.6}$$

where $tb_e > 0$, $tb_y < 0$ and $tb_y{}^\star > 0$. In addition, it is necessary to impose assumptions on domestic interest-rate determination. For the small open economy, with capital mobility, the domestic interest rate is fixed to a common world rate. If, however, capital mobility is zero, then the interest rate continues to be determined domestically and the closed economy results, derived above, remain valid.[2]

Although the external sector does not affect the solution of the above model for the interest rate under zero capital mobility, fiscal actions do have important implications for the real exchange rate. In order to keep the trade account in balance following a fiscal expansion, the exchange rate will have to rise in order to discourage the excess domestic demand from raising imports (or at least ensure that exports rise by enough to offset any increase in imports). There is again a differential between the effects of spending increases and tax cuts, with tax cuts only affecting private expenditure (and the exchange rate) when they are viewed as permanent, or if people have a positive marginal propensity to consume out of temporary changes in income.

In this static model, the introduction of perfect capital mobility (and asset substitutability),[3] ensures the domestic interest rate is tied to the foreign rate and therefore held fixed in the comparative statics. Equations (3.6) and (3.2) can now be solved for the level of domestic income and the exchange rate. For a bond-financed tax cut the exchange response is

$$\frac{d_e}{-d^r} = -\frac{c_y}{tb_e} < 0 \tag{3.7}$$

which says that the exchange rate will now appreciate by just enough to crowd out the expansionary effects of fiscal policy on domestic expenditure. The solution is particularly simple because income is now determined (given the real money stock) by the interaction of the foreign interest rate with the LM schedule. With income fixed, the IS schedule alone ensures goods market equilibrium through changes in the exchange rate. This simple static model makes clear that capital mobility is a crucial determinant of the exchange-rate response to budget deficits; under zero capital mobility the exchange rate depreciates; and under high capital mobility it appreciates. This is the first example of the income-expenditure model's ability to explore simple financial market hypotheses with much greater ease than the intertemporal models discussed above.

Incorporating wealth into the perfect capital mobility case is also straightforward. The rate of interest is again tied to the foreign rate, leaving the exchange rate to equilibrate the goods market. The exact response of the exchange rate is given by

$$\frac{de}{dg} = \frac{(1 - c_y - tb_y)m_w + m_y(1 + c_w)}{m_y tb_e} < 0. \tag{3.8}$$

Again, incorporating wealth into the model reinforces the transactions effects of deficits on financial markets. The rise in perceived wealth raises domestic consumption (adding to the increased transactions demand for money) and directly raises money demand via the expansion of the private sector's portfolio of assets. With interest rates fixed, the rise in money demand must be offset in the goods market via an appreciation which dampens the rise in domestic absorption, and generates a trade deficit.

The Mundell–Fleming model can also be easily extended to the more realistic case of flexible prices, as was done by Argy and Salop (1979). Indeed, for the analysis of interest and exchange rates, the basic conclusions go through with fixed output and perfectly flexible prices or with some combination of output and price flexibility. In the example with zero capital mobility (the closed economy equivalent) a fiscal action which raises private absorption, either directly or by stimulating private sector spending, puts upward pressure on prices, lowers real money balances and, with income fixed, this must lead to a rise in the rate of interest. The portfolio effects of issuing more government bonds to finance the deficit again reinforces this indirectly by raising consumption and directly by raising money demand. In the open economy, with prices flexible, it is now important to distinguish between nominal and real exchange-rate movements. For the zero capital mobility case, the rise in prices generated by the fiscal expansion would imply a loss of competitiveness (and a trade deficit) unless the nominal exchange rate rises. There must again be a depreciation, although this time of the nominal rather than the real exchange rate. The analysis is also little changed when capital is perfectly mobile. The fiscal expansion puts upward pressure on prices and the interest rate, but with the interest rate fixed (along with M and y) the price level cannot rise and incipient capital inflows appreciate the exchange rate as before.

The final extension of the static Mundell–Fleming model is to the two-country case. There are few unexpected results from this extension. Tax cuts raise world interest rates by raising the demand for goods produced in both countries. The exchange rate will generally appreciate in the home country following a fiscal expansion, but this requires the assumption that the home country has a higher propensity to consume its own goods relative to the foreign good. The two-country model was originally discussed by Mundell (1968), but more general results are given in Mussa (1979).

Before summarizing the results so far it is worth pointing out that there are many other extensions of the static framework outlined above. Some of the most widely recognized extensions include: the inclusion of a real exchange-rate effect in the private consumption function (Laursen and Metzler 1950); the deflation of wealth by a consumer price index rather than by the price of domestic output; and the separation of nominal and real interest rates in the money-demand and investment functions. All of these extensions are included in Marston (1985), where it is shown that they do not qualitatively alter the static results, although they do have important implications for stabilization policy. Some of these modifications will be discussed in more detail in the analysis of dynamics.

To conclude this subsection, it is worth highlighting the key issues that come out of the simple static Mundell–Fleming model, as the simpler models tend to provide the clearest testable hypotheses. First, there is the question of capital mobility or openness. As capital mobility rises, the classic closed economy hypothesis that deficits cause higher interest rates is undermined (at least for the small economy). In its place, however, is the equally strong hypothesis that deficits lead to an appreciation of the exchange rate. A second issue is the fact that deficits resulting from government spending should have different (much stronger) effects on financial markets than deficits caused by cutting taxes; the possibility was suggested that a tax cut may have no effect on private sector spending, so that permanent wealth effects of higher debt would need to be important for a one-period tax cut to have a strong influence on interest and exchange rates. The last point that should be mentioned is that the analysis has not incorporated any dynamics. Once the role of expectations, stock adjustments and intertemporal budget constraints are included, the static results must be qualified. It is to these issues that we now turn.

The dynamic Mundell–Fleming model

During the 1970s the Mundell–Fleming model came under attack from a wide range of critics. In particular, the trend toward freely floating exchange rates and the rapid rise in inflation led many to question the absence of any role for expectations in the model. This critique was damaging because of the incomplete definition of equilibrium in the Mundell–Fleming framework. As has already been pointed out, the static model ignored the fact that asset stocks may adjust slowly following an exogenous shock, implying dynamic feedback on the important endogenous variables. Those who originally developed the model realized this limitation, but denied its relevance to their short-run stabilization analysis (see Mundell 1968, p. 271). Unfortunately, if agents are rational and forward-looking, then expectations of future dynamics will play an important role in the determination of the short-run impact effects of stabilization policy. There have been two distinct reactions to this criticism from mainstream economists. The first reaction, following the recommendations of the 'New-Classical School', has returned to the micro-foundations of macroeconomics to build models based on individual optimization principles, usually within intertemporal frameworks, such as was examined in Chapter 2. The second approach has been to adjust and extend the basic model to incorporate many of the missing dynamic adjustment mechanisms. These extensions are the topic of the rest of this chapter, with most attention being paid to the dynamic behaviour of the exchange rate.

One of the most important and early extensions of the Mundell–Fleming model was the inclusion of the uncovered interest parity condition,

$$r_t = r_t^\star + E(\dot{e}_t), \tag{3.9}$$

which allows the domestic interest to deviate from the external rate according to expected changes in the exchange rate, as in Dornbusch (1976). The Dornbusch model was used to examine monetary policy and does not incorporate wealth effects or the dynamics of asset accumulation. A fiscal expansion, therefore, produces the same results as in the static model; an appreciation and no change in the interest rate or the level of income.[4]

For a realistic analysis of fiscal policy, at least two more dynamic equations must be added to the Mundell–Fleming model to capture dynamic adjustment. First, the budget constraints of the government sector:

$$\dot{b}_t = \bar{g}_t + r_t b_t - \tau_t. \tag{3.10}$$

Second, a net foreign asset equation,

$$\dot{nfa}_t = tb_t + r_t^* nfa_t, \tag{3.11}$$

which says that foreign bonds are accumulated via current account surpluses, in turn composed of both the trade and service account balances. The definition of wealth must also incorporate net foreign assets, that is,

$$w_t = m_t + b_t + nfa_t.$$

Full steady-state equilibrium can only occur when equations (3.10) and (3.11) are set to zero, along with exchange-rate expectations in equation (3.9). In the long run, the interest rate is again fixed to the foreign rate, although it can vary during the adjustment process to offset expected changes in the exchange rate. The long-run solution for the exchange rate is of particular importance, as it anchors the dynamic path of both the interest rate and the exchange rate, regardless of how expectations are formed. The long-run solution for a fiscal expansion in many models is for a depreciation of the currency — the opposite result obtained in the static model, although the results do require the imposition of a priori constraints on relative parameter magnitudes.

A key assumption concerns the relative size of the wealth effects in the absorption and money demand equations. As is shown in Branson and Buiter (1983), the removal of the wealth argument from the money-demand equation can produce an appreciation even in the long run. In contrast, models that emphasize wealth in the money demand equation (Dornbusch and Fischer 1980), find the real and nominal exchange rates depreciating in the long run. Intuitively, the second view seems most attractive. We have seen that, in the short run, a budget deficit is associated with a deficit in the trade account. Over time the trade deficit will lead to a reduction in net foreign assets from equation (3.10). Initially, the wealth effects of lower net foreign assets may be offset by the higher level of bonds in the hands of the private sector and possible valuation effects (if the exchange rate appreciates on impact).[5] However, both of these offsets must be temporary and real wealth must fall in the long run. There are two main mechanisms whereby falling wealth can equilibrate the current account (that is, produce a stable solution). First, the decline in wealth can directly reduce absorption and the trade deficit if the marginal propensity to consume out of wealth is positive. Second, the decline in wealth can reduce the demand for money, putting downward pressure on interest rates, leading in turn to a depreciation and an improvement in the trade account. Depending on which of the above effects is emphasized, it is possible to obtain either a rise or fall in the real exchange rate in the long run. A formal analysis of these issues is undertaken in Penati (1983).

The short-run dynamic response of the exchange rate is determined in conjunction with the interest rate. In almost all models the interest rate responds to the short-run goods-market pressures and rises on impact. The exchange rate must then depreciate over the course of adjustment according to the dynamics specified in equation (3.9). Whether the exchange rate rises or falls on impact depends on both the long-run steady-state position of the exchange rate and the elasticity of exchange-rate expectations. In the case where the exchange rate appreciates in the long run, it must also appreciate in the short run (and overshoot its steady-state value). In the case of a long-run depreciation, there can be an appreciation or depreciation depending on the speed of adjustment to the new steady state and the specific features of the model. In all cases there is a current account deficit, falling real interest rates and a depreciating exchange rate during the adjustment process.

Imperfect asset substitutability

The development of portfolio balance theory led many authors to question the relevance of the perfect asset substitutability hypothesis used in the early open economy literature. In one of the earliest pieces, Branson *et al.* (1977) showed how intervention in the foreign exchange market could influence real exchange rates by altering the relative supplies of foreign versus domestic interest-bearing assets. This early analysis neglected goods markets and had only limited relevance to the fiscal policy debate. In recent years, however, the portfolio balance insights have been incorporated into the dynamic Mundell–Fleming model producing a number of interesting modifications.

The addition of imperfect asset substitutability into the Mundell–Fleming model requires, at a minimum, the separation of the demand functions for domestic and foreign interest bearing assets:

$$b_t = b(r_t, r_t^\star, E\dot{e}_t)W_t, \tag{3.12}$$

$$nfa_t = f(r_t, r_t^\star, E\dot{e}_t)W_t; \tag{3.13}$$

which can be rewritten in a format more comparable to the uncovered interest parity assumption used above:

$$r_t = r_t^\star + E\dot{e} + \omega(\ldots), \tag{3.14}$$

where the ω function may be defined simply as a risk premium (as in Branson 1985; 1986; Branson *et al.* 1985) or as a more complicated function of both asset preferences and capital mobility (as in Sachs and Wyplosz 1984). Either way, the implication of equation (3.14) is that there may be a role for the interest rate to vary in response to domestic factors, as was the case in the closed economy and zero capital mobility literature discussed above.

Branson (1985) outlines a relatively straightforward model in which the asset demand functions are similar to equations (3.12) and (3.13), output is fixed at full employment, and prices are flexible. Dynamics are included by adopting rational expectations in the asset demand functions and through a net foreign asset accumulation equation similar to equation (3.11). There is no dynamic budget constraint in the model so a fiscal expansion must be interpreted as a balanced budget rise in spending or as a one-period deficit. The Branson model produces the same general results as the interest parity models discussed above, that is, an impact appreciation and current account deficit induced by higher consumption and the associated rise in interest rates. Over the adjustment path there is a depreciation because the current account deficit reduces the outstanding stock of net foreign assets and, therefore, the demand for assets denominated in the domestic currency.

This similarity in results arises via somewhat different channels, and is not robust to extensions and generalizations of the portfolio balance model. Sachs and Wyplosz (1984) have shown that, depending on the composition of government spending, the exact degree of asset substitutability, and the initial size of asset holdings, the exact opposite results to Branson (1985) can be produced; that is, a long-run appreciation of the exchange rate combined with a short-run depreciation.

Sachs and Wyplosz (1984) paper also contains a dynamic equation for the government's budget constraint allowing a more complete analysis of the effects of government debt on interest rates and exchange rates. Not surprisingly, the model also simplifies in other directions, most notably by omitting the monetary sector altogether. Moreover, the introduction of a dynamic equation for the supply of domestic bonds makes the analytical solution of the model unmanageable; comparative dynamics is done through numerical simulations. It is, however, an important contribution to the fiscal deficit literature as it is one of the only open economy models to incorporate a dynamic role for debt-financed deficits.

One of the most important features of the Sachs–Wyplosz model is the careful specification of the dynamic budget constraint. In particular, they recognize that deficits cannot be financed indefinitely by selling bonds to the private sector (see also Christ 1979). Eventually, the burden of interest payments will necessitate the elimination of the deficit through higher taxes or via reduced spending. This is formalized through a simple policy-reaction function,

$$\dot{b}_t = \mu(\bar{b} - b_t), \tag{3.15}$$

where $\bar{b}$ is a target sustainable level of debt and μ is an adjustment coefficient. By substituting equation (3.15) into the budget constraint (equation (3.10)), the interrelationships between the fiscal policy instruments is highlighted. In the case of a tax cut, (holding g constant), we can derive the following reaction function,

$$\tau_t = -\mu\bar{b} + (\mu + r_t)b_t. \tag{3.16}$$

The implication of equation (3.16) is that a tax cut generates dynamics in both the bond stock and taxes. Taxes must rise during the adjustment phase to finance interest payments and to eliminate the fiscal imbalance (according to equation (3.15)). Moreover, if there is a rise in the target level of debt, a tax cut will imply a long-run fiscal contraction as taxes must rise above their initial steady-state level in order to finance a larger steady-state interest burden.

The analysis of a tax cut within this framework is particularly interesting, as it provides some insight into the relative importance of expenditure and financial channels. The long-run solution for a tax cut depends on three factors: the depressing effect of higher steady-state taxes on spending; the expansionary effects on spending from higher government debt (and wealth); and the portfolio balance effects of a higher stock of government bonds on interest rates (which reduces spending). If this last effect dominates, that is, if assets are not highly substitutable, then the long-run result will be a rise in the rate of interest and an appreciation of the currency. In this case, the exchange-rate appreciation results because absorption is lowered enough to produce trade account surpluses and a rise in net foreign assets over the adjustment phase. This leads to a long-run improvement in the service account that must be offset by the appreciation. When asset substitutability rises there is less of a portfolio balance effect on interest rates and more likelihood of a long-run depreciation, as was the case in the Branson (1985) type models.

In contrast to the long run, the impact effects of a tax cut lead to a short-run depreciation when substitutability is low. The expenditure and wealth effects now both work towards an appreciation, but the portfolio effect of a rise in the domestic bond stock is to raise the rate of interest, depress the exchange rate and induce a trade surplus. The dynamic path now involves a falling exchange rate and current account surpluses. The appreciating exchange rate occurs despite a positive interest differential (that would suggest that the exchange rate is expected to rise), because portfolio balance effects dominate exchange-rate expectations in the dynamic determination of the domestic interest rate, as is seen in equation (3.13). There are also intermediate cases, where the exchange rate appreciates slightly on impact, and shows a long-run appreciation as well.

In the Sachs–Wyplosz simulations the initial bond stocks are set to zero to avoid valuation effects of exchange-rate changes on asset stocks and interest payments. This is not important in the small-country framework, but has been shown by Kole (1985) to be important when the model is extended to the two-country case. Fiscal policy now affects interest rates in both countries. If each country holds the other's bonds, then any change in the interest differential has direct implications for the service component of the current account. Exchange-rate changes complicate the dynamics further by adding a valuation effect on top of this interest differential effect. Without discussing all the possible permutations of the Kole two-country model, it is worth stressing that the conventional results presented above may be moderated and even reversed for a high enough degree of asset market integration. Valuation effects can dominate expenditure and portfolio effects in the short run and service accounts dynamics may dominate trade-account dynamics in the long run.

Some extensions

The above models impose assumptions that are, in some cases, somewhat restrictive. To examine how important these assumptions are for the results discussed, this section examines briefly some attempts to extend the Mundell–Fleming model by relaxing such assumptions as the flexibility of prices and the homogeneity of domestic output. The analysis remains within the portfolio balance framework as this still contains the perfect substitutability model as a special case.

The first extension is the addition of a supply side to the model, which allows dynamics in both prices and output. Adding a simple Phillips curve to the Sachs–Wyplosz model does not qualitatively alter their results, but does lead to a higher exchange rate on impact; it has almost no effect on the rate of interest. This is also confirmed by Argy (1986), who provides even more detail on the supply side (as well as a detailed monetary sector). Although Argy does not examine alternative substitutability parameters, and does not incorporate a dynamic budget constraint, his model produces a short-run appreciation and long-run depreciation — following a balanced budget expansion. The rate of interest rises on impact but falls over the adjustment phase until it returns to its original steady-state level.

The final extension is the use of the traded and non-traded goods approach in a dynamic framework, as first examined by Genberg and Kierzkowski (1979). Their model contains no discussion of the government budget constraint and is therefore not well-suited to the analysis of budget deficits. However, it does highlight the need to distinguish between alternative classes of goods in the economy. If, as in Genberg and Kierzkowski (1979), the model includes a non-traded good (whose price is set internally), along with traded goods (whose prices are determined on world markets), then a shift in government expenditure from traded to non-traded goods will appreciate the real exchange rate (now defined as the relative price of the two sets of goods). The appreciation holds both in the short and the long run. The short-run appreciation results from a rise in non-traded goods prices, rather than a fall in the nominal exchange rate. In the long run, the rise in the price level lowers real wealth and absorption, creating a current account surplus and appreciating the nominal exchange rate and the real rate even further.

Testable hypotheses

It is now possible to draw together some general conclusions that follow from the Mundell–Fleming model and its extensions, and to compare them with the results that were obtained from the intertemporal models. The first point to note is that the closed economy framework again produces very simple and clear-cut hypotheses to be tested. A rise in government debt should raise interest rates via both expenditure and portfolio channels; this result is common to both Chapters 2 and 3 as long as the conditions for debt neutrality are not met. The second point is that the closed economy results soon break down once capital mobility is allowed for. Interest rates are then determined on world markets and are not effected by domestic fiscal policies. For the small open economy, the crucial financial market variable that now adjusts to a debt shock is the domestic currency, which appreciates. Factors that dampen, and even reverse, the impact appreciation (the presence of rational expectations; lower asset substitutability; and flexible income) all do so by putting upward pressure on the rate of interest. Any empirical test of the effects of deficits in a multi-country model must clearly be a joint test on interest and exchange rates.

Another factor, common to many of the dynamic models, is that the impact effects are often reversed once the dynamic adjustment of asset stocks commences. If the exchange rate appreciates on impact, then it generally depreciates over the adjustment phase, and vice versa. Similarly, after rising on impact, the interest rate usually falls during the dynamics of adjustment. This last point needs to be qualified in the case of low asset substitutability, when the interest rate may rise even further if there is a dynamic budget constraint in the model. Finally, the inclusion of non-traded goods opens up an additional channel for the expenditure effects of a deficit to place downward pressure on the exchange rate in the long and the short run. Again this conclusion is consistent with the intertemporal models, at least once restrictions have been placed on relevant consumption parameters.

Finally, in both chapters it was argued that deficits may impact on financial markets directly by raising the stock of outstanding debt. This effect, which is separate to the flow effects of deficits, will operate even if agents fully anticipate the higher future taxes needed to service the larger debt stock.

These theoretical conclusions will be used in the remainder of this book to guide empirical investigations. However, before proceeding to the empirical results, the following chapter examines how other researchers have attempted to test for the effects of deficits and debt in financial markets.

Notes

1. In particular, it may be possible to use debt policy to manipulate the term structure of interest rates by swapping government bonds at differing maturities.
2. This correlation between the closed economy IS/LM model and the zero capital mobility version of the IS/LM model will be taken up in more detail in Chapter 5.
3. It will be assumed that domestic and foreign bonds are perfect substitutes in the following two subsections.
4. See Devereux and Purvis (1984) for further discussion of the role of fiscal policy in the Dornbusch-type model.
5. The valuation effects occur because the definition of wealth now includes net foreign assets. The direction of this effect can go either way depending on the sign of net foreign assets.

Part II
Empirical Issues

Chapter 4

Empirical work to date

Introduction

The empirical literature on the role of government debt in financial markets is both large and diverse. It can be divided into two general fields. The first, using largely single equation techniques, is devoted to testing explicitly the Ricardian Equivalence Theorem. It is one of the most controversial areas of research in empirical macroeconomics. Despite the importance of open economy considerations in the determination of financial market responses to fiscal deficits, the majority of empirical work in this field has employed closed economy assumptions, bypassing altogether the issue of international interdependence and exchange-rate effects. These international linkages are increasingly being stressed in the theoretical work, as was seen in the previous two chapters.

The second field is related to the estimation of larger macroeconomic systems. These large multi-country models do include detailed linkages between goods and financial markets, but often take for granted that deficits and debt have real effects. Because these models generally are not set up to test for Ricardian equivalence, they tend not to be useful for exploring the role of debt in financial markets. They are also so large that interpreting simulation results is not a straightforward task. Exceptions are the small special-purpose models that have recently become popular. These try and reduce the complexity and generality of the multi-country model, with the aim of testing only one or two hypotheses. Although somewhat less controversial, this area is rather underdeveloped, particularly in regards to international applications.

The aim of this chapter is to review both strands of the empirical literature; highlighting key unresolved issues, rather than presenting and comparing all existing results. It begins with a brief review of the alternative single-equation models that have been used to test explicitly the Ricardian Equivalence Theorem. These include: consumption function tests; interest-rate tests; and reduced-form exchange-rate tests. It then reviews the role of fiscal policy in multi-country models. A final section draws together the outstanding issues that remain unresolved and suggests likely strategies for the following empirical chapters.

The main conclusions from the chapter are that the Ricardian Equivalence Theorem remains an unresolved issue requiring further empirical investigation. It is argued that progress on determining the role of government debt in financial markets has been hampered by the neglect of international fincancial market integration. Two directions of research are suggested: the first should incorporate the assumption of asset-market integration by looking at the world financial system as a complete whole; the second approach suggested is to develop further the small special-purpose multi-country models. These can be specified to ensure that strong tests of the Ricardian hypothesis can be made within a complete structural system.

Reduced-form tests

The consumption function

Both the intertemporal models of Chapter 2 and the traditional models of Chapter 3 indicated that one possible direct effect of increased government debt is higher private sector consumption. It is, therefore, not surprising that the consumption function has been one of the primary test vehicles in the Ricardian debates. Table 4.1 provides a summary of the results obtained in this literature. This is not supposed to be an exhaustive list, but is rather a selection from some of the better-known journals; no attempt has been made to present one particular approach or another. There is no general conclusion to be drawn from these results. Support for the Ricardian result is obtained in just about half of the cases.

Table 4.1 Consumption function tests

Authors	Country	Results
Kochin (1974)	USA	Support hypothesis
Feldstein (1982)	USA	Reject hypothesis
Seater (1982)	USA	Support hypothesis
Koskela and Viren (1983)	9 countries	Reject hypothesis
Kormendi (1983)	USA	Support hypothesis
Boskin and Kotlikoff (1985)	USA	Mixed results
Knight and Masson (1985)	3 countries	Reject hypothesis
Van Wijnbergen (1986b)	'World'	Reject hypothesis

Note: The above indications as to whether results support or reject the Ricardian hypothesis are based on the authors' own interpretations of their results.

Moreover, there is no tendency for this ambiguity to be eliminated over time. Recent studies continue to provide mixed results.

Explaining these contradictory results is difficult. In a number of cases the consumption-function specifications are very similar. For example, the studies of Feldstein (1982) and Seater (1982) both employ very broad specifications, including almost all possible channels for government policy to impact on consumption. Both use a similar time horizon and US data. Estimation techniques, which were perhaps a problem in the early literature, were both two-stage least squares to allow for simultaneity problems. Feldstein rejects the Ricardian hypothesis, while Seater claims to find strong support for it. One possible explanation for the paradox is that data definitions are not identical. This is a particularly large problem in any fiscal policy test because published data are rarely used directly in the empirical work; it is normally manipulated or even generated by the researcher to be consistent with the theory.[1]

A second explanation for the paradox is the multicollinearity problem caused by including a wide range of fiscal policy variables in each test equation. In many tests, the equations contain the entire government budget constraint, ensuring almost perfect collinearity among the explanatory variables. This argument is supported by the fact that the few studies that employ very simple consumption functions, with only a few key fiscal variables, tend to reject the Ricardian hypotheses (see, for example, Knight and Masson 1985).

A third problem with much of this literature is the fact that it ignores international linkages. As shown by Sachs and Wyplosz (1984), a fiscal deficit may actually lower absorption in an international setting when domestic bonds are imperfect substitutes for foreign bonds. This result occurs despite the fact that bonds are considered as part of the private sector's net wealth. Intuitively, the wealth effects are swamped by portfolio effects.[2]

The final problem with the consumption-function approach was raised in Chapter 2 in discussing the intertemporal effects of deficits and debt. It was argued there that the intertemporal effects of higher debt show up primarily in the private sector's asset-demand functions; the flow and stock effects in the consumption function are likely to be small and perhaps statistically difficult to pick up. However, even if there are no, or very small, effects in the consumption function, this does not mean that higher debt will not have real effects via the asset demand side. Carmichael (1984) provides empirical support for this proposition from an estimated capital stock equation.

Interest-rate equations

The easiest way to overcome the last criticism of the consumption-function

Table 4.2 Interest-rate tests

Authors	Country	Results
Sargent (1969)	USA	Reject hypothesis
Feldstein and Eckstein (1970)	USA	Reject hypothesis
Echols and Elliot (1976)	USA	Mixed results
Plosser (1982)	USA	Support hypothesis
Makin (1983)	USA	Support hypothesis
Mascaro and Meltzer (1983)	USA	Support hypothesis
Blanchard and Summers (1984)	OECD	Support hypothesis
Evans (1985)	USA	Support hypothesis
Tanzi (1985)	USA	Reject hypothesis
Hoelscher (1986)	USA	Reject hypothesis
Merrick and Saunders (1986)	10 countries	Support hypothesis
Feldstein (1986b)	USA	Reject hypothesis
Barro (1987a)	UK	Support hypothesis
Evans (1987a)	USA	Support hypothesis
Evans (1987b)	6 countries	Support hypothesis

Note: The above indications as to whether results support or reject the Ricardian hypothesis are based on the authors's own interpretations of the results. In the case of Tanzi, it has subsequently been pointed out that he misinterpreted the sign on the deficit variable. See comments in *IMF Staff Papers*, 1987.

approach is to incorporate both the asset-market and goods-market effects of deficits and debt in the one reduced-form interest-rate equation. In this approach, the IS and LM functions are both solved together for the interest rate, leaving a reduced-form equation that contains a wide variety of exogenous variables, including both government spending and its various methods of financing.

A summary of the results for this literature is in Table 4.2. It is not supposed to be an exhaustive list, but a representative selection of work that is often quoted. There is no agreement here on the role of deficit financing in interest-rate determination. The controversy is again present across countries and over time, (although nearly all work has been concentrated in the United States). The reasons for this controversy may again be associated with data problems and model specification. The reduced-form test equations tend to be somewhat similar to those used in the consumption-function literature, and, as mentioned above, there is a wide variety of fiscal variables and data sources available to the econometrician. Most of the test equations also contain a large number of fiscal variables which may produce problems of multicollinearity for the reasons outlined above.

Apart from the above problems that are common to all methods of testing the Ricardian Equivalence Theorem, there are a number of other problems associated directly with the interest-rate approach. First, the interest-rate equations employed in many tests are not always strictly reduced-form tests in that they contain endogenous variables such as income and inflation. Although recent tests have tried to correct for simultaneous equation bias, many of the early studies (and some recent studies) used simple ordinary least squares (see, for example, Feldstein and Eckstein 1970; Hoelscher 1986).

Second, the theory says that the dependent variable in these tests should be the real interest rate, not the nominal rate. One therefore needs a measure of the real interest rate, something that must be constructed. Unfortunately, there is no agreed method for doing this. Each researcher has different preferences on the derivation of the real interest rate. The general picture obtained from alternative measures is unlikely to be very different, as is shown in Atkinson and Chouraqui (1985) and Blanchard and Summers (1984); however, measurement error may be introduced into the estimations, undermining the power of the test. This is particularly true for those studies using finely sampled data. The work of Merrick and Saunders (1986) attempts to reduce this noise by averaging the measurement errors in inflationary expectations, something that will also be employed in the empirical chapters below. Similarly, there are many different interest rates that can be used in the test equations: Short-term versus long-term; private versus public, and so on. While generalizations are difficult, it appears that those studies employing long-term interest rates tend to be the ones finding a relationship between interest rates and deficits; those employing very short-term rates tend to accept the Ricardian hypotheses.[3] One explanation for this is that short-term interest rates, being highly volatile and determined primarily in money markets, are (like exchange rates) very difficult to model.

A third problem in this literature relates to the fundamental objectives of the researchers. In many cases the aim does not appear to be to test the Ricardian Equivalence Theorem as set out in Chapter 2, but to explore the role of budget deficits in financial markets. This often leads to the omission of important explanatory variables. In particular, many test equations (see Feldstein 1986b); and Hoelscher (1986) do not include government-spending variables. It is then impossible to tell whether deficits cause higher interest rates because of tax illusion or because of higher government spending.

A final explanation, stressed throughout this book, is that most interest rates are determined in integrated international asset markets and yet the empirical work to date invariably uses closed economy models to derive reduced form tests. A major implication of this (derived formally in Chapter 5), is that both national and world fiscal policy variables are important determinants of the level of interest rates in any country that is open to international capital movements. It is not possible to test for the effects of domestic debt on domestic interest rates without including international linkages into the analysis. The only reduced-form studies that explicitly incorporate this open economy aspect are Blanchard and Summers (1984) and, more recently, Evans (1987b). In Blanchard and Summers (1984) a world fiscal policy index is constructed. However, no formal empirical work is carried out using this index, as it only runs from 1978 to 1984. They argue that because there appears to be little rise in the index in the early 1980s, fiscal policy is not to blame for rising world interest rates over that time. I would argue that the index does not fully capture the stock effects of rising public debt, but concentrates too heavily on the flow efects of deficits. For this reason it does not show the extent of the fiscal stimulation that has occurred at the world level since the mid-1970s.

Evans (1987b), published after the present research was largely completed, does point out the importance of international financial market linkages and uses a reduced-form equation that is quite similar to the one derived in Chapter 5. However, because he does not derive his results by summing up the individual economies that comprise the world economy, he makes a number of mistakes in the empirical implementation of his equation. The most important is the omission of any cross-country linkages between interest rates and exchange rates — the interest-parity relationship. This would not be a problem if he estimated his world model directly. In fact, he just estimates interest-rate equations for the major economies as a system, and imposes equal coefficients across countries. His empirical technique is also very suspect for reasons discussed in the following section.

The alternative to looking at aggregated world interest rates is to estimate a structural multi-country model that incorporates international linkages. Such methodology is discussed in the final sections of this chapter.

Exchange-rate equations

The open economy literature on the effects of fiscal policy on real exchange rates is much smaller and much more fragmented than the closed economy consumption function and interest-rate literature discussed above. Empirical work has, until very recently, concentrated on monetary models of exchange-rate determination at the expense of fiscal policy. Over the last five years, however, there has been a number of papers exploring the role of budget deficits and debt in the open economy. Among these, there are a few that address real exchange-rate effects of fiscal policy.

One of the earliest studies to introduce explicitly the theoretical linkages between real interest and exchange rates was Sachs (1985) who estimated a simple real exchange-rate equation based on the uncovered interest-parity condition. Sachs found that real interest differentials were able to explain a substantial proportion of the movement in the dollar–Deutschmark real exchange rate over the 1978–84 period. More importantly, the use of relative 'fiscal impulse' measures, as instruments for real interest rates, improved the overall fit of the equation and raised the explanatory power of the interest differential. The Sachs results are only suggestive that deficits may be important in determining real interest and exchange rates. He was in no way explicitly testing the importance of deficits and debt in exchange-rate determination. Moreover, his results do not seem to be robust to extensions of his time period or to other countries (See Camen and Genberg 1986). There are three major problems with Sachs's model which may explain why it does not generalize outside his data set. First, he does not derive the model from a macroeconomic structure, so that the final reduced form may suffer from missing variables to a large extent. Second, and related to the first point, there is no allowance for simultaneity between the determination of the exchange rate and the interest rates. Finally, the model does not incorporate the possibility that domestic and foreign bonds may be imperfect substitutes, thus breaking the interest parity link. (This is probably most important for countries other than the United States and West Germany.)

Many of these problems were addressed by Weiller (1984), where a reduced-form real exchange-rate equation was derived from a standard Mundell–Fleming model, with portfolio balance asset-demand schedules. The results were mixed and somewhat difficult to interpret because it was not possible to extract the structural coefficients from the reduced forms. At the same time, the equations did confirm that both fiscal deficits and debt do seem to be important determinants of real exchange rates, although there was considerable variation across countries in regard to the importance and sign of the effects. This result is consistent with the theoretical results derived in Chapter 3, where it was shown that asset substitutability, initial debt positions and various other country-specific characteristics would determine both the impact and dynamic response of the real exchange rate to fiscal shocks. Weiller's most interesting and intuitively plausible conclusion is that fiscal deficits tend to appreciate the US dollar on impact. For the other countries the results are not as strong or consistent, but here is some suggestion that higher debt and larger deficits may cause real depreciations, especially in the smaller industrial countries of France, Italy and Canada.

More recently there have been two studies published on deficits and exchange rates that have opened up more Ricardian controversy. Evans (1986) provided evidence that the US budget deficit had nothing to do with the US dollar appreciation up to 1985, while Feldstein (1986a) provided evidence arguing exactly the opposite. These two studies are worth examining briefly because they typify the alternative approaches to examining the role of deficits in financial markets. Neither study derives a reduced form explicitly from a structural model, but both end up with similar equations containing deficit, money and inflation variables. As above, Feldstein (1986a) does not incorporate a government-spending variable, so is not a proper test of Ricardian equivalence. In contrast, Evans (1986) does include a government spending variable. Once this is included, however, the deficit variables generally indicate that a US deficit leads to a depreciation of the dollar.

Apart from the inclusion of a government-spending variable, the two studies also adopt different approaches to handling the forward-looking nature of financial markets. Feldstein obtains actual forecasts of future budget deficits and uses these as proxies for expected future deficits. Although this approach suffers from the criticism of being *ad hoc*, the explanatory power of his equation is relatively high for exchange-rate models. Evans uses the rational expectations assumption and argues that it is only unexpected movements in exogenous variables that drive exchange rates. He then takes the residuals from a vector-auto-regression as proxies for unexpected movements in exogenous variables and employs them in the test equation. The approach (dating back to Plosser 1982 and also used in Evans 1987b) appears to be a rather shaky methodology for hypothesis testing. It assumes, in the construction of the exogenous variables, that the market does indeed operate the way the economist models it. In this case, one must believe that the market uses only a five variable vector-auto-regression system to make forecasts of exogenous variables. Given the errors that must be introduced in the first stage of variable construction, the methodology can have little reliability and seems especially suited to rejecting the hypotheses. In fact, by imposing rationality in the construction of the data, one is ruling out a major possible source of non-neutrality that is the object of the test.[4]

More generally, all of the above single-equation exchange-rate tests suffer from two major theoretical problems. The first issue was raised in Chapter 2, when deriving the intertemporal effects of a permanently higher level of government debt. It was argued there that the flow, or one-period impact of higher debt, that is, via the deficit, is likely to be small compared to the permanent stock effects of a one-period deficit. The implication is that it is likely to be the debt stock (rather than the deficit) that is most important for any empirical work on financial markets. Despite this, all the above studies concentrate only on the effects of deficits and ignore the role of government debt. This suggests that further empirical work on the role of government debt may provide more conclusive results than those results obtained so far looking only at deficits.

Second, from the theory of Chapters 2 and 3, it should be remembered that, in almost any model containing a reasonable amount of structural detail, there will be an ambiguous sign on the debt of deficit variable in a reduced-form exchange-rate equation. In other words, both the results of

Feldstein and Evans may be evidence against the Ricardian Equivalence Theorem, as they both found significant effects of deficits on exchange rates (although of opposite signs). The crucial point is that it is necessary to derive test equations from a structural model and even then it may not be possible to draw strong conclusions. This final point is a major motivation for the estimation of more detailed structural models that can distinguish between wealth and portfolio effects of deficits and debt. These models are discussed in the following section.

Multi-country models

To obtain greater insight into the structural coefficient on key fiscal variables and to examine the dynamic adjustment process, one clearly needs models with more structural content than the reduced-form approach. There are two alternatives. An obvious one is to simulate existing large multi-country models to obtain fiscal policy multipliers. This has been done by Hooper (1985), Sachs (1985), Amano (1986) and Frankel (1986). The other is to estimate small highly simplified multi-country models which can be used directly for hypothesis testing, as well as for dynamic policy simulation. This is the approach taken in Knight and Masson (1985) and Haas and Masson (1986). Both of these approaches are reviewed briefly, although more attention is given to the second group of models, which are likely to be of greater relevance to the present work.

Large multi-country models

There are a large number of multi-country models that have become operational since the mid- to late 1970s. They are now an accepted tool in almost all areas of empirical international macroeconomics. However, the objective in building large multi-country models is generally not to test a single hypothesis. They are expensive and time-consuming to construct and maintain. Such expense can only be justified if they have application to a wide variety of issues, normally related to forecasting and policy analysis, rather than hypothesis testing. The aim of this section is not to try to evaluate the results of all the major multi-country models. Rather, it is hoped to point out some of the more general conclusions that can be drawn from them, and especially to highlight the difficulties of using such models to evaluate specific hypotheses, such as the Ricardian Equivalence Theorem.

To isolate the importance of public sector debt in financial markets it is necessary to simulate a multi-country model for a permanent increase in the level of government debt. Unfortunately, nearly all the published

Table 4.3 Second-year fiscal impact in multi-country models

Models	US variables			Currency value	Non-US variables		
	CPI	R	CA		CPI	R	CA
Expansion in the USA							
MCM	0.4	1.7	−16.5	2.8	0.4	0.4	8.9
EEC	0.6	1.5	−11.6	0.6	0.2	0.3	6.6
EPA	0.9	2.2	−20.5	1.9	0.3	0.5	na
LINK	0.5	0.2	−6.4	0.1	0.0	na	1.9
Liverpool	0.2	0.4	−7.0	1.0	0.6	0.1	3.4
MINIMOD	0.3	1.1	−8.5	1.0	0.1	0.2	5.5
OECD	0.6	1.7	−14.2	0.4	0.3	0.7	11.4
Expansion in the non-US Block							
MCM	0.2	0.5	7.9	0.3	0.3	0.6	7.2
EEC	0.1	0.0	3.0	0.6	0.8	0.4	−9.3
EPA	0.3	0.6	4.7	−0.7	0.7	0.3	na
LINK	0.0	0.0	6.3	−0.1	0.1	na	−6.1
Liverpool	3.1	0.8	11.9	3.3	0.8	0.0	−17.2
MINIMOD	0.2	0.3	3.2	0.6	0.2	0.9	−2.2
OECD	0.2	0.3	3.3	0.9	0.7	1.9	−6.9

Notes: *CPI* is the percentage change in the consumer price index, *R* is the change in the level of the nominal short-term interest rate, Currency value is the percentage change in the domestic value of a weighted exchange rate (a positive number is an appreciation), and *CA* is the change in the current account in billions of dollars. The models are described in Frankel (1986).

studies on fiscal policy multipliers in multi-country models report the effects of government-spending based fiscal expansions. This makes it impossible to distinguish between the expansionary flow effects of higher government spending and the stock effects of higher government debt. Despite this limitation, it is still worth briefly looking at what are the standard results that come out of the major models from a fiscal policy expansion.[5] In Table 4.3 a summary of fiscal multipliers is provided for some of the best-known multi-country models. The table has to be taken directly from Frankel (1986, p. 20), who reports the results of a comparative Brookings Institution study. The usefulness of this study is that all model-builders tried to use the same baselines and implement the same fiscal expansions.

The first unambiguous result from the simulations is the positive and strong effect on government-spending-induced deficit on nominal interest rates. Moreover, all models indicate that the rise in interest rates is also positively transmitted to the rest of the world, that is, world interest rates unambiguously rise following a fiscal expansion in either the United States or the non-US bloc. The current account responses are also unanimously of a negative sign, as expected according to conventional economic theory.

The exchange-rate responses, in contrast, depends, at least in some models, on the origins of the fiscal shock. When the expansion occurs in the United States, all models predict an appreciation of the US dollar, supporting the reduced form results obtained by Feldstein. However, if the expansion is in the non-US bloc, then a number of models point to a home-currency depreciation — the low capital mobility (or asset substitutability) result.

A major problem with the results presented in Table 4.3 is that they represent only the multipliers taken at a particular (*ad hoc*) point in time, during what may be a complex non-monotonic adjustment path. If one is to determine the consistency of the theoretical results obtained from conventional macro-models, then it is necessary to look at the entire adjustment path. One of the important conclusions from Chapter 3 was that the impact and long-run solutions to a fiscal shock may be of opposite signs. This problem is highlighted if one looks at the comparative study presented in Amano (1986). In this study four of the large models are shocked in a similar fashion to the fiscal experiment conducted above. In this case, the unambiguous results, of the US deficit appreciation the US dollar, no longer apply. In the MCM and the OECD models, the US dollar appreciates on impact and then depreciates over the long run. In contrast, the EPA and LINK models show an impact depreciation followed by a gradual appreciating. It is a mere coincidence that all four models happen to show an appreciation after two years. In other words, the typical fiscal policy simulations carried out using the most accepted multi-country models do not provide a particularly clear picture for the exchange-rate response, although most models do agree that deficits do lead to higher interest rates.

In recent years there has been a strong desire to try and explain the 1980-5 US dollar appreciation by simulating multi-country models, the results obtained both by Sachs (1985) and Hooper (1985) do tend to confirm that a portion of the US dollar appreciation can be explained by the imbalances in the stance of international fiscal policy. Futhermore, as theory would suggest, the expansion of the US deficit was also responsible for part of the rise in world interest rates and the deterioration of the US current account. A major problem with these simulations is that it is impossible to determine what proportion of the results derive from the inevitable model adjustments, required to ensure a stable (or believable) baseline, and what proportion reflects the true estimated relationships. In the case of the Sachs model, which is not estimated, there can be no sense in which the results can be used to test the theoretical hypotheses raised in the previous sections. Even when the models are fully estimated, as in the case of Hooper (1985), the key equations linking countries together — especially the exchange-rate equations — are usually modified for the purpose of the policy simulation. Indeed, without modification Hooper admits that the Federal Reserve's MCM could not have tracked the dollar's appreciation up to 1985. Another problem with these simulations is the fact that it is very difficult to sort out why and how the results are generated. This is not a criticism of the models as such, but simply means that, for the purpose of hypothesis testing, it is impossible to distinguish between the expenditure effects and portfolio effects of the simulated deficits.

Special-purpose multi-country models

An alternative to simulating existing large multi-country models is to estimate small special-purpose systems that are specified to capture the essential dynamic effects of deficits and debt accumulation on financial markets. Because these models are designed for specific purposes, they are more useful for exploring particular hypotheses. Such an approach is of course very common in other areas of macroeconomics, where it is often necessary to substitute out large sections of a structural model leaving only the most relevant components. In the area of multi-country modelling there have been only a few recent attempts to build small special-purpose models and, as far as I know, only one, Knight and Masson (1985), which was designed to examine fiscal policy issues.[6] There has, however, been a tendency in recent years to develop mini-versions of the large multi-country models that are both easier to handle and the results of which are easier to understand. Of these, MINIMOD is perhaps the best known; its fiscal policy results will be discussed in some detail.

Knight and Masson reduce the world to a system of four countries (the United States, Japan, West Germany, and the rest of the world) with only four estimated equations for each — savings, investment, export and import functions. Fiscal policy enters the model only via wealth effect on savings, and this effect is rigorously estimated to allow the data to determine the importance of tax discounting. Their results point to partial, but incomplete, discounting of expected future taxes. This partial myopia in the savings function ensures that deficits do raise real interest rates at home, and because there is no role for differing degrees of asset substitutability, the exchange rate appreciates on impact. The initial appreciation impacts on the export and import functions and sends the current account into deficit; this in turn runs down domestic holdings of foreign assets and reduces wealth. In the long run net foreign assets are reduced substantially, requiring a depreciation of the currency to offset the weakness in the current account induced by lower interest income. The interest rate (which is a world rate) rises both on impact and in the long run, as the theory would suggest.

Although the Knight and Masson model gives substantial insights into the wealth effects of government debt, and seems to provide a reasonable explanation of the 1980–5 appreciation of the dollar, it lacks any financial markets and therefore could not be expected to pick up the possible portfolio balance effects of higher debt. It is not surprising that the model predicts exactly the same pattern of adjustment for the other countries' fiscal expansion as it does for the US debt shock — impact appreciation and long-run depreciation. This is the only possible exchange-rate response in a non-Ricardian world with capital mobility and perfect asset substitutability. If one believes in the possibility that international financial markets may have portfolio preferences with regard to the type of assets they hold, then it is necessary to extend the type of model estimated by Knight and Masson to include a financial market sector.

MINIMOD (see Haas and Masson 1986; and Masson 1986) does have a financial market sector, along with much more detail in other sectors as well.[7] It, too, does not allow for imperfect asset substitutability, as interest and exchange rates are linked via the interest-parity condition. The fiscal policy simulations are, as a result, very similar to those reported by Knight and Masson. The exchange-rate appreciates on impact and depreciates over the adjustment path for both US and non-US fiscal expansions.

MINIMOD also allows for fiscal policy to impact on other areas of the economy. In particular, it includes government spending in the absorption function. This ensures that the fiscal shocks reported (they are in fact spending shocks) cannot be seen as being a test of the Ricardian Equivalence Theorem. Some very simple simulations of tax cuts using MINIMOD, however, appear to produce very similar results to those for spending increases.[8] This non-Ricardian result is not surprising as MINIMOD has a tax-discounting parameter, but it appears to have been arbitrarily fixed in all simulations. MINIMOD, at least as it stands, is therefore not a particularly useful means of testing the role for tax discounting and the effects of government debt in general. However, it does highlight the usefulness of small models for special-purpose analysis. This is because one of the main purposes of MINIMOD was to explore the implications of the rational expectations hypothesis in a multi-country model. All the fiscal policy simulations are reported using both rational and adaptive expectations solution procedures. The results conform to theory in that the exchange rate (both for fiscal and monetary shocks) is much more volatile under the rational than under the adaptive expectations assumption. Under adaptive expectations, both the exchange rate and interest rates move very little on impact. This contrasts to the Knight and Masson analysis, where it is shown that it makes only quantitative differences to the results if one employs static rather than rational expectations.

Conclusions and further extensions

Is it now possible to draw together some general conclusions about the impact of debt and deficits on real interest and exchange rates? Their effect on real interest rates should be the easiest to disentangle, yet the empirical evidence based on reduced-form interest-rate equations remains controversial, to say the least. This controversy, I have argued, may stem largely from measurement and specification problems and the failure to consider open economy constraints in the reduced-form analysis.

Once one does move to the open economy literature, there is a much greater occurrence of a positive link between deficits and real interest rates. Unfortunately, there are very few cases in this literature where it is possible to ascertain whether it is higher government spending or higher level of debt that is generating the higher interest rates. The interest-rate–deficit link clearly requires further empirical work, especially in the open economy framework.

Given the uncertainty surrounding the deficit–interest-rate link it is not surprising that the deficit–exchange-rate link is also an undecided one. The reduced-form evidence does suggest that deficits play an important role in exchange-rate dynamics, but the importance of this effect appears to be country-specific and the theoretical mechanisms at work are not clear from the types of empirical analysis generally undertaken. The evidence is certainly strongest in the case of the United States, where deficits almost always raise the real interest rate and put pressure on the dollar to appreciate in the short run.[9] It should be added that the evidence of the United States is heavily weighted by studies of the most recent period of fiscal expansion; it would clearly be useful to examine other historical periods, including the era of fixed nominal exchanges rates. For the other industrial countries, the evidence is too scanty and inconsistent to make any general statements. It may, in fact, turn out that for many countries there is no stable relationship between deficits and exchange rates; again further empirical work is needed before any strong claims can be made.

To conclude, it is now possible to outline a number of areas where further work is needed to try and sort out some of the unresolved issues raised in this chapter. In terms of theoretical structures employed, it seems likely that the extended IS/LM type model (or parts of it) will remain the most popular one for empirical analysis. This reflects the fact that the alternative — to derive models based on individual optimization — has not yet reached the point where there is an accepted international macro-model that falls out of this analysis. At the same time, there is clearly a need to incorporate the dynamic insights of the intertemporal approach in empirical work on deficits, given that the primary role of deficits is to transfer income and spending intertemporally. The approach of Knight and Masson (1985), which allows the data to determine the importance of the Ricardian Equivalence Theorem, provides a useful example of this kind of methodology. Another area that requires further empirical attention is the importance of permanent stock effects of large budget deficits on financial markets. The work to date has concentrated on the politically sensitive area of deficits themselves, and this has led to the neglect of the medium-term effects of sustained deficits on the level of debt. If the theory of Chapter 2 is correct, then it is the stock effects of higher debt that are likely to be much more important for financial markets than the flow effects of deficits.

In terms of specific topics, there is a number of areas that stand out as requiring further attention. One is the role of deficits and public debt in the world economy as a whole. Although such an approach raises problems of aggregation, it solves many of the complications that arise when modelling inter-country linkages such as exchange-rate equations and current account dynamics. It also avoids the problem of modelling international policy reactions, a problem that is generally ignored in the empirical literature.[10] World-economy aggregation appears to be the only clean way to test a simple reduced-form interest-rate equation, without running into problems of missing variables and/or multicollinearity. For these reasons, Chapter 5 will be devoted to deriving and implementing a powerful test of the Ricardian Equivalence Theorem based on an aggregated model of the world economy.

A second area that requires attention is the exploration of the role of asset substitutability and capital mobility in determining the real exchange-rate response to fiscal policy in both the short and long run. For this issue some sort of multi-country model is obviously required. As discussed above, the very large multi-country models are not well suited to this task because they have not been designed for hypothesis testing and are almost impossible to 'see through'. I believe that the most useful approach will be to construct 'special-purpose' models that capture the essential channels through which fiscal policy operates, while leaving much of the macroeconomy unspecified. This is the approach to be taken in Chapter 6.

Notes

1. There is no agreement on the appropriate measures of fiscal stance and particularly of public sector deficits and debt. At least two issues must be decided before utilizing fiscal data: first, the definition of the public sector; and second, adjustments necessary to published nominal data (see Buiter 1985 where these issues are outlined). A common mistake in much of the Ricardian literature is the use of nominal deficits without allowing for the effects of the inflation tax on the stock of debt.
2. This is likely to be a major problem for studies using medium and small-sized economies, such as Koskela and Viren (1983).

3. See, however, Evans (1987a) where both short and long-term rates are found to be unrelated to deficits. His analysis ignores the recent US debt expansion, which may help explain his findings.
4. See also Feldstein (1986b) and Poterba and Summers (1987), where the limitations of this empirical technique are discussed.
5. It should be recalled that in nearly all theoretical models examined above, the qualitative responses of interest rates and exchange rates to both tax cuts and rises in government spending were very similar.
6. There have been a number of small simulation models built using non-estimated coefficients, but these are of limited value for hypothesis testing. See, for example, Eichengreen and Wyplosz (1986) and Frenkel and Razin (1987).
7. Depending upon the exact specification, the model contains around 70 equations. This is still quite small compared to the large multi-country models. The Federal Reserve's MCM, for example, uses over 900 equations when fully linked.
8. Because taxes and debt are endogenous in MINIMOD it is not easy to engineer a permanent tax cut or debt increase. The experiment I conducted was to reduce the tax rates in MINIMOD (parameters UT1 and UT2 in the description given in Haas and Masson 1986).
9. The major exception to this is the reduced form work of Evans (1986).
10. See, however, Oudiz and Sachs (1984) where multi-country models are explicitly used to address issues of policy coordination.

Chapter 5

World interest rates

Introduction

The previous chapter raised serious questions about the validity of testing the Ricardian Equivalence Theorem using closed economy assumptions in a world that is becoming more and more interdependent. It was argued that much of the existing empirical literature, being based on closed economy assumptions, but applied to individual economies, does not reflect recent theoretical advances in the analysis of fiscal policy in an international setting. In particular, the literature, reviewed in Chapters 2 and 3, has shown that international linkages are of vital importance in determining the response of domestic financial markets to fiscal deficits and debt policy when capital mobility is high.

The aim of this chapter is to explore how one might incorporate the possibility of highly integrated asset markets into a test of the Ricardian hypothesis. Using a very simple n-country model, it is shown below that the closed economy framework is only suitable for testing the Ricardian Equivalence Theorem in individual economies if one assumes the presence of low or zero asset substitutability or capital mobility.[1] Under the more usual hypothesis of capital mobility, this chapter demonstrates formally that interest-rate tests of Ricardian equivalence should incorporate international linkages. An alternative, a conceptually much simpler, solution is to remain within the closed economy framework, but extend the scope of empirical work to the world economy, that is, to the determination of the world interest rate. The second approach, used in this chapter, has number of advantages: first, it allows one to stay within the well-known closed economy theoretical models (the alternative open economy extensions, being more recent, remain relatively controversial); second, it allows one to use the huge existing empirical literature, on the determination of interest rates in the closed economy, as a base to compare results and econometric techniques; third, it avoids the complex and unresolved issues of how to model exchange rates and exchange-rate expectations; and finally, it should, as argued by Merrick and Saunders (1986), reduce the errors in variables problem associated with measuring expected real interest rates.

The chapter opens with a brief description of the theoretical framework employed. The main aim here is to derive a reduced-form interest-rate equation that basically conforms to the income-expenditure models outlined in chapter 3, but which is capable of providing a strong test of the Ricardian Equivalence Theorem. This is done by including wealth and portfolio balance effects in the consumption and money-demand functions. A brief description of the data is then provided, followed by a presentation of the empirical results. The first part of this presentation looks at interest-rate determination and the Fisher hypothesis in the world economy; the second compares results from the real interest-rate equations, both for the 'world' as whole and for individual countries. Appendix B extends the work of this chapter by incorporating the dynamics of capital accumulation into a 'world' model.

There are three main conclusions from the chapter. The first is that there are strong theoretical reasons to doubt tests of Ricardian equivalence based on individual country interest-rate equations using closed economy models. Second, both nominal and real interest-rate equations for the 'world' as a whole show significant positive coefficients on government debt, providing no support for the Ricardian Equivalence Theorem. The estimations point to rising 'world' debt as being responsible for a large portion of the rise in world real interest rates which has occurred in the 1980s. Third, the 'world' interest-rate equations perform substantially better than the individual country equations, suggesting that international capital markets are closely integrated. Even for large countries there are improvements in explaining domestic real interest rates if foreign variables are employed in estimation. Many of these results will be used in Chapter 7 when the role of deficits and debt in policy coordination is examined.

The theory

A general framework

This subsection sets out a general framework that is consistent with the traditional income-expenditure models used in most of the empirical work surveyed in Chapter 4. The model is a static real model containing no price adjustment or capital accumulation; Appendix B provides a simple extension including a capital accumulation equation and the dynamics of adjustment are explored. To emphasize the importance of open economy considerations for testing the Ricardian Equivalence Theorem, the model of the 'world' economy is developed from the individual open economy.

Table 5.1 List of notation

a	=	private absorption
$\bar{y}_d$	=	expected disposable income
y	=	real output
w	=	real wealth
r	=	real interest rate
e	=	real exchange rate (a rise in e represents a depreciation)
τ	=	real taxes
nfa	=	net foreign asset position
tb	=	trade balance (in domestic currency)
ca	=	current account (in domestic currency)
m	=	real money
b	=	real bonds
g	=	government spending on goods
res	=	central bank reserves
E	=	forward expectations operator

Notes: Capital letters refer to nominal variables and small letters refer to real variables. Stars refer to foreign variables. The starred foreign variables can be thought of as an aggregated rest-of-the-world, but are more accurately described as a vector of the $n-1$ foreign country variables. Dots represent time derivatives and a bar over a variable indicates its long-run steady-state level. The subscript d denotes demand for a variable and the subscript s denotes exogenously given supply of a variable.

The model contains n identical small open economies each made up of two sectors; the goods market, represented by the IS curve; and the financial markets, represented by the open economy LM curve. These are represented by standard functional relationships in equations (5.1) – (5.6) (with notation explained in Table 5.1).

$$y = a + g + tb(y, y^\star, e) \tag{5.1}$$

$$a = f(w, \bar{y}_d, r) \tag{5.2}$$

$$w = m + b_s + nfa \tag{5.3}$$

$$m_s - m_d(r, r^\star, E\dot{e}, y)w = 0 \tag{5.4}$$

$$b_s - b_d(r, r^\star, E\dot{e})w - eb_{d\star}(r, r^\star, E\dot{e})w^\star = 0 \tag{5.5}$$

$$g = \tau + \dot{b} + \dot{m} - \dot{res} \tag{5.6}$$

The following subsection derives linear reduced-form interest-rate equations that will be used in the empirical analysis.

The IS curve (for the ith country) is derived from the usual income-expenditure identity (5.1). Each country produces a composite domestic good that is consumed or invested according to equation (5.2), or exported to the foreign countries. The absorption function is similar to that derived from the intertemporal literature where Ricardian equivalence does not hold.[2] The important implication from this specification is that deficits (increased debt) will have a direct wealth effect on consumption and indirectly put upward pressure on interest rates. The other important point to note is that absorption is a function of steady-state or expected lifetime income, rather than actual disposable income. This removes the flow effects of deficits on absorption from the model (i.e. taxation) and leaves only the stock effects of changes in debt. It was the stock effects that the previous chapter emphasized as being the most likely reason for Ricardian equivalence not to hold, but which are often excluded from empirical models.

The financial market sector is represented by equations (5.3) to (5.5); a portfolio balance setting. Domestic residents hold a portfolio of three assets, comprising domestic money (non-traded), a domestic bond (traded), and foreign bonds. The demand for each asset is a function of total wealth and the vector of rates of return on the alternative assets, as in the Tobin (1969) framework.[3] Money, which is used as a means of exchange, is also a function of domestic income. The domestic demand function for net foreign assets is not shown and is not required to solve for the domestic interest rate.

Equation (5.6) is the government's temporal budget constraint. It requires that government expenditure be financed by taxes, deficits (b), printing real money or running down foreign exchange reserves. It is included as a reminder that the government is constrained as to the number of instruments available. Although it has five instruments, only four are linearly independent, and for most countries the use of reserves is not a permanent source of government finance. The main empirical implication is that any reduced-form test that includes government spending and all its forms of financing, will suffer from near perfect multicollinearity.

The reduced form

In this section reduced-form interest-rate equations are derived for the individual small economy and for an aggregate 'world' economy. The IS curve is obtained by substituting equations (5.2) and (5.3) to give (after linearization),

$$y_t^i = \gamma_0 + \gamma_1 m_t^i + \gamma_2 b_t^i + \gamma_3 b_t^\star - \gamma_4 r_t^i + \gamma_5 g_t^i + \gamma_6 e_t^i + \gamma_7 y_t^\star. \quad (5.7)$$

As in the extended Mundell–Fleming model, aggregate demand is a positive function of all financial assets, government spending, the exchange rate and foreign income; it is a negative function of the real interest rate.

Following Tobin (1969), the real interest rate can be written as a function of all asset stocks and the alternative rates of return. By substituting equation (5.3) into equation (5.4) one obtains

$$r_t^i = \delta_0 - \delta_1 m_t^i + \delta_2 b_t^i + \delta_3 b_t^\star + \delta_4 y_t^i + \delta_5 (r_t^\star + \dot{E} e_t^i). \tag{5.8}$$

An increase in the money stock reduces the real rate; a rise in the stock of government bonds raises the interest rate, the coefficient on foreign bonds is ambiguously signed, although it will be positive if foreign assets are closer substitutes for bonds than for domestic money; income has a positive effect on interest rates via the transaction demand for money; and finally, the return on holding the foreign bond also has a positive coefficient. Equations (5.7) and (5.8) can be solved to obtain the final real bond-rate equation.

$$r_t^i = \phi_0 - \phi_1 m_t^i + \phi_2 b_t^i + \phi_3 b_t^\star + \phi_4 g_t^i + \phi_5 e_t^i + \phi_6 y_t^\star + \phi_7 (r_t^\star + \dot{E} e_t^i),$$

$$\tag{5.9}$$

where

$$\phi_0 = \frac{\gamma_0 \delta_4 + \delta_0}{1 - \gamma_4 \delta_4}; \qquad \phi_1 = \frac{\gamma_1 \delta_4 + \delta_1}{1 - \gamma_4 \delta_4}; \qquad \phi_2 = \frac{\gamma_2 \delta_4 + \delta_2}{1 - \gamma_4 \delta_4};$$

$$\phi_3 = \frac{\phi_3 \delta_4 + \delta_3}{1 - \gamma_4 \delta_4}; \qquad \phi_4 = \frac{\gamma_5 \delta_4}{1 - \gamma_4 \delta_4}; \qquad \phi_5 = \frac{\gamma_6 \delta_4}{1 - \gamma_4 \delta_4};$$

$$\phi_6 = \frac{\gamma_7 \delta_4}{1 - \gamma_4 \delta_4}; \qquad \phi_7 = \frac{\delta_5}{1 - \gamma_4 \delta_4}.$$

Equation (5.9) is an appropriate test vehicle for examining the effects of fiscal policy on real interest rates for any individual open economy. It could be estimated as it stands, or the real exchange rate could be substituted out, using equation (5.5.) and some specification of expectations formation. Unfortunately, both these approaches are difficult without an adequate theory of real exchange-rate determination and/or without a measure of expected changes in real exchange rates. It also requires using foreign variables — the bond stocks and foreign income — which substantially increases the size of the data collection task, just to perform a simple static reduced-form test. Because of these difficulties, most tests of the Ricardian Equivalence Theorem have ignored the open economy theoretical considerations and employed the closed economy model of interest-rate determination in individual economies.[4]

However, as pointed out above, the closed economy model is only applicable to the individual country when we have zero (or near zero) capital mobility. In this case, the trade balance is always zero (dropping out of the IS curve); while foreign asset stocks and interest rates are no longer relevant for the home country's financial markets (dropping out of the LM curve). In this extreme case it is possible to rewrite equation (5.9) as;

$$r_t^i = \phi_0 - \phi_1 m_t^i + \phi_2 b_t^i + \phi_4 g_t^i, \tag{5.10}$$

which is the conventional closed economy, reduced-form interest-rate equation generally applied in the Ricardian literature.[5] Using equation (5.10), however, means relying heavily on the assumption of zero capital mobility, an assumption that is increasingly questionable for any of the major industrial economies.

An alternative to relying on the zero capital mobility assumption embodied in equation (5.10), or to using the more complex (but more general) specification in equation (5.9), is to go back to the original IS and LM equations and specify a model for the world economy as a whole. Rewriting the IS and LM equations (5.7) and (5.8) as averages of all n countries gives

$$y_t^w = \gamma_0 + \gamma_1 m_t^w + \gamma_2 b_t^w - \gamma_4 r_t^w + \gamma_5 g_t^w, \tag{5.11}$$

and

$$r_t^w = \delta_0 - \delta_1 m_t^w + \delta_2 b_t^w + \delta_4 y_t^w, \tag{5.12}$$

where the superscript w represents the averaging of the n individual countries so that

$$X^w = \frac{1}{n} \sum_{i=1}^{n} (X^i).$$

Notice that the trade balance drops out of equation (5.11) as the world does not (as yet) trade beyond its borders. Similarly, the expected exchange-rate changes are eliminated in equation (5.12).

Solving equations (5.11) and (5.12) gives us the world economy reduced-form interest-rate equation

$$r_t^w = \phi_0 - \phi_1 m_t^w + \phi_2 b_t^w + \phi_4 g_t^w. \tag{5.13}$$

This equation has the same testable coefficients as both (5.9) and (5.10), but can be estimated efficiently, and without bias, using ordinary least squares. It does not require the estimation of exchange-rate expectations or any international interest-rate linkages.

Despite the obvious attractions of using equation (5.13) to test the Ricardian Equivalence Theorem, a number of limitations must be kept in mind. First, the aggregation of individual country data requires the assumption of equal cross-country coefficients; i.e. identical structure in each country. This is clearly a strong assumption (given variation in institutional structure across countries) and it must be kept in mind when interpreting the results.[6]

A second limitation relates to the aggregation of financial assets. By summing up all outstanding bond stocks, the model explicitly assumes that domestic and foreign bonds are close substitutes. The model is therefore unable to throw light on the question of asset substitutability and the role of budget deficits in generating international interest-rate differentials. Such issues must be addressed within the framework of equation (5.9), the individual open economy model, and are left for Chapter 6.

The empirical analysis will concentrate on the estimation of the reduced-form, closed economy equations (5.10) and (5.13). These equations will be used to test two main hypotheses (although other interesting issues do arise). First, the main concern is to determine the importance of public debt in the determination of real interest rates; this involves testing for a positive significant ϕ_2. The second hypothesis to be tested relates to the role of capital mobility in interest-rate determination. If the hypothesis of zero or low capital mobility is true (which is the Feldstein and Horioka 1980 view), then individual country estimates based on equation (5.10) should perform as well as, or better than, the aggregate model posed in equation (5.13). If, however, capital mobility is relatively high, then the individual economy equations should provide little explanatory power, especially for the smaller industrial countries. In particular, the individual country equations should suffer from missing variables bias, ensuring inaccurate coefficient estimates, low Durbin–Watson statistics (if the missing variables are serially correlated) and low $\bar{R}^2$ statistics.

Before implementing the above models there is the question of how to measure the long-term real interest rate, given that inflationary expectations are unobservable. The approach taken here is to use the Fisher identity,

$$r = R - E\dot{P}_C, \tag{5.14}$$

which says that the real interest rate is equal to the nominal rate (R) minus the expected rate of inflation (EP_C).[7] This can be substituted into the primary test equations (5.10) and (5.13) to give (dropping the superscripts)

$$R_t = \phi_0 - \phi_1 m_t + \phi_2 b_t + \phi_4 g_t + \phi_8 E\dot{P}_{C_t}. \qquad (5.15)$$

The coefficient ϕ_8 should be insignificantly different from unity under the very strict version of the Fisher identity. Equation (5.15) will then be used to compare the performance of the most commonly employed proxies for inflationary expectations. The equation can also be used to see if the other coefficients are sensitive to alternative measures of expectations.

It should be noted that many previous studies of the Fisher hypothesis have been unable to find a unit coefficient on the expected rate of inflation. One explanation (of many) for this is that proxies of EP_C contain measurement errors which bias the regression tests unless good instruments can be found to correct for the errrors in variables.[8]

This problem may be largely overcome, as has been shown by Merrick and Saunders (1986), once one aggregates over a large number of countries if the mean error in measured inflationary expectations is zero and if the cross-country errors are not highly correlated. Assuming the above conditions hold, then, as the number of countries gets larger, the average measured inflation error will get smaller as positive and negative errors cancel each other out. If an adequate measure of inflationary expectations can be found, it can be taken over to the left hand side of equation (5.15) allowing the estimation of the hypothesized real interest-rate model.

The current account of the OPEC countries (in real US dollars) was also used in the estimation procedure as an exogenous variable (labelled op).[9] This was introduced to capture one important exogenous shock to world interest rates not included in the theoretical model. The justification for including this variable is that our data base does not cover the 'world' as specified in the model. By including OPEC's current account position it is hoped to capture a major exogenous shock to the world's financial system that would otherwise not be reflected in the exogenous variables. The hypothesis to be tested is that OPEC's marginal propensity to consume out of its current account surplus is much lower than the OECD's. As a result, the large OPEC surpluses in 1973–4 and in 1979 should have resulted in an excess supply of world savings and lowered the world real interest rate.

The other important external shock to the OECD financial system was the debt crisis. No attempt has been made to allow for this as it cannot be argued that the debt crisis was an exogenous shock. An interesting extension of the model would be to include the LDC block explicitly, as has been done by Van Wijnbergen (1986b). He found strong effects running from real world interest rates to LDC debt problems. It is interesting to note that he also rejects the Ricardian Equivalence Theorem using the OECD consumption function as a test equation.

The data

Given that the aim of the model is to capture the determinants of 'world' interest rates, the primary objective in setting up a data base was to incorporate as many of the major industrial countries that have comparable data on the variables required. To achieve this aim it was necessary to use annual data (from 1960 to 1985) and to ignore a number of country-specific institutional factors in favour of cross-country consistency.

The final data base includes twelve of the largest OECD countries, comprising around 90 per cent of the total OECD (based on GNP weights). Wherever possible data were taken from the IMF's International Financial Statistics (IFS) tape, although a number of series had to be updated, backdated or constructed from separate domestic sources. A complete listing of the data and sources is provided in Appendix A; however a brief description of sources may be useful

The nominal interest rate is a long-term government-bond yield. The money stock is the IFS narrow money; the debt variable is private sector holdings of central government debt,[10] and the government-spending variable is government consumption of goods and services on a national accounts basis. For each country these three policy variables were all deflated and scaled by dividing through by trend nominal GNP in each country.[11] Inflation is the annual change in consumer prices.

The first measure of inflationary expectations employed is a backward-looking measure derived from adding the coefficients of a fourth-order polynomial distributed lag. The second measure is forward-looking. It is an average of the current and following year's actual inflation rates. Being unobservable at time t when market rates are determined, this measure clearly suffers from measurement error that will end up in the disturbance term. A key assumption in the estimation is that such measurement errors are not serially correlated and have a zero mean. The final measure of expectations is a combination of the first two. It is a centred moving average of the past, current and following year's inflation rate.[12]

The aggregation of the individual twelve countries' data into world variables was done using GNP shares as weights. Variable weights were used to reflect the substantial changes in relative sizes of the major economies over the period. (Japan's weight rose from 4 per cent in 1960 to 16 per cent in 1985). For the endogenous variable (the real interest rate) an average of the weights was employed to avoid criticism that the weighting scheme might introduce spurious correlation between the right and left-hand-side variables. In fact, a number of different weighting schemes were tried to check the sensitivity of the results and, in all cases, the key results carry through.

The results

Debt neutrality and the Fisher hypothesis

Table 5.2 reports the results of the estimation of the nominal and real interest-rate equations for the aggregated models, equations (5.13) and (5.15). The first three sets of coefficients reflect the three different measures of inflationary expectations. For the distributed lag specification, the coefficient on inflationary expectations, at 0.735, is reasonably close to unity,[13] and much higher than in many of the studies discussed above. The fit of the equation is good, with an $\overline{R}^2$ value of 0.93. The Durbin–Watson (DW) statistic is in the indeterminate range, but not excessively low. The coefficient on the money stock is negative and significant. The coefficient on the debt variable (ϕ_2) is significantly positive, providing no support for the Ricardian Equivalence Theorem. The OPEC current account variable (*op*) has the expected significant negative sign. The only insignificant variable is government spending, which also has the wrong sign.

The use of the forward-looking measure of inflationary expectations provides much less explanatory power, as reflected by the rise in the SE statistic for that equation.[14] The signs on all coefficients remain unchanged in the second equation, but the standard errors rise. Finally, the mixed measure of inflationary expectations provides very strong

Table 5.2 Reduced-form 'world' interest-rate equations

Measure of expectations	Estimated coefficients					Statistics		
	m	*b*	*g*	*op*	EP_C	$\overline{R}^2$	SE	DW
Backward[a]	−58.692	13.445	−0.443	−0.034	0.735	0.93	0.671	1.45
	(8.785)	(4.170)	(25.563)	(0.024)	(0.122)			
Forward[b]	−66.292	27.323	−17.809	−0.103	1.182	0.82	1.089	1.53
	(13.359)	(10.441)	(45.949)	(0.047)	(0.352)			
Mixed[c]	−64.942	19.792	−13.564	−0.037	0.838	0.96	0.527	1.38
	(6.536)	(4.098)	(2.709)	(0.015)	(0.120)			
Real rate	−61.498	24.420	−36.823	−0.052	–	0.94	0.561	1.62
	(6.405)	(2.360)	(13.928)	(0.011)	–			

Notes: Figures in parentheses are standard errors. Constant terms were estimated in all equations.

a Expected inflation is a fourth-order third-degree polynomial lag on past inflation. The coefficient reported is the sum of the lagged coefficients.
b Expected inflation is an average of the current and following year's inflation rate.
c Expected inflation is a centred moving average of the previous, the current and the following year's inflation rates.

support for the theoretical model. The Fisher hypothesis cannot be rejected (at the 95 per cent level), the SE of the equation is lower than for all other equations, and the *t*-statistic on all variables are the highest. The coefficients on all the variables (except government spending) support the model of equation (5.15) at conventional significance levels.

Given the support of the Fisher hypothesis present in Table 5.2, especially in the equation using the 'mixed' measure of expectations, the inflationary expectations variable was taken over to the left-hand side of the equation to estimate the real interest-rate models of equation (5.13). The results of this estimation are presented in the last line of Table 5.2, using the mixed measure of inflationary expectations. Not surprisingly, the coefficients are very similar to the nominal interest-rate equations, except that the standard errors are even lower on most of the coefficients. The Ricardian Equivalence Theorem is again strongly rejected. The model suggests that, of the 6½ percentage-point rise in the world real interest rate that occurred between 1979 and 1984, the rise in real government debt was responsible for almost half.

The only unusual result from the model is the persistent negative sign on the government spending variable (now significant). It was initially thought that this negative sign may result from the fact that the expenditure measure was not cyclically adjusted and may be negatively correlated with income (which should be positively related to the interest rate). To check for this, a two-stage estimation was carried out, treating government spending as a partly endogenous variable. As can be seen from the top line of Table 5.3, this estimation made no fundamental difference to the results so was not pursued.

Another possible explanation relates to our theoretical model. Mankiw (1986) shows that the inclusion of durable consumption goods in a macro-model can produce a negative relationship between government spending

Table 5.3 Adjusted real interest-rate equations

Adjustment	Estimated coefficients				Statistics		
	m	*b*	*g*	*op*	$\bar{R}^2$	SE	DW
Endogenous *g*	−65.221	26.834	−56.891	−0.043	0.94	0.588	1.51
	(7.071)	(2.834)	(18.879)	(0.013)			
No *g*	−54.666	19.990	–	−0.068	0.92	0.633	1.61
	(6.610)	(1.874)	–	(0.013)			
No *b*	−41.210	–	65.541	−0.121	0.66	1.35	1.21
	(14.713)	–	(23.663)	(0.021)			

Note: Figures in parentheses are standard errors. Constant terms were estimated in all equations.

and the real interest rate (something which he argues is a very common result in the empirical literature). Frenkel and Razin (1986c) also show how the composition of government spending can affect the relationship between spending and the real interest rate. Finally, the negative sign may have resulted from either multicollinearity between the exogenous variables, or from aggregation bias. To ensure that neither of these problems had infected the other coefficient estimates, the model was also estimated without the government expenditure variable and then in turn without the debt variable. The results are also in Table 5.3. The omission of the government-spending variable does not affect greatly the performance of the model, although it does lose some of its explanatory power; the coefficient on the debt variable changes little and becomes even more significant. In contrast, the equation without debt performs much worse than all the others. The $\bar{R}^2$ falls dramatically, as does the DW statistic. At the same time, the coefficient on government spending changes sign and is now significant, suggesting that multicollinearity is the cause of the negative sign in the fully specified model. These sensitivity results provide even more support to the argument that it is the stock and portfolio effects of higher debt that are more likely to lead to higher real interest rates, than the flow effects of taxes and government spending.

Capital mobility

Table 5.4 contains the results for the individual countries under the null hypothesis of zero, or low, capital mobility, that is, equation (5.10). If this hypothesis is correct, then the individual country equations should also provide strong support for the model. In particular, the $\bar{R}^2$ statistics should not fall dramatically and the DW statistics should continue to show a lack of serial correlation. If, however, the capital mobility hypothesis is correct, then the individual country equations should suffer from missing variables bias; they should show much lower explanatory power, the presence of serial correlation in the errors, and bias and inconsistent coefficient estimates.

A quick glance at the $\bar{R}^2$ and DW statistics in Table 5.4 will confirm that the individual country estimations do not support the low capital mobility hypothesis. Even for the United States, the explanatory power of the model is much lower, and the hypothesis of serially correlated errors cannot be rejected. Given that the individual country equations appear to be misspecified, the estimated coefficients are likely to be biased and do not provide a useful test of the debt-neutrality hypothesis. Further evidence of bias coefficients is provided by comparing a simple average of the individual coefficients with the 'world' model. In most cases, the average of the country results is very different to the 'world' results. At

Table 5.4 Real interest-rate equations

Country	Estimated coefficients				Statistics		
	m	*b*	*g*	*op*	$\bar{R}^2$	SE	DW
United States	−59.805 (12.795)	33.730 (5.923)	−4.965 (35.406)	−0.069 (0.019)	0.84	1.047	1.09
West Germany	−72.926 (13.311)	3.041 (2.853)	−22.901 (7.258)	−0.023 (0.010)	0.78	0.455	1.49
Japan	−20.905 (14.937)	11.477 (5.309)	−116.861 (76.313)	−0.055 (0.055)	0.67	2.602	0.59
France	−15.731 (11.812)	10.758 (9.728)	6.806 (29.831)	−0.077 (0.026)	0.39	1.542	1.07
United Kingdom	−75.087 (37.646)	20.982 (8.217)	10.375 (7.768)	−0.127 (0.029)	0.59	1.723	1.13
Italy	−18.656 (9.001)	6.014 (7.730)	19.932 (37.457)	−0.123 (0.042)	0.58	2.172	0.83
Canada	−12.503 (13.496)	20.846 (4.792)	−2.091 (2.209)	−0.052 (0.023)	0.65	1.289	0.954
Australia	30.060 (44.167)	−8.309 (35.090)	36.429 (22.486)	−0.153 (0.042)	0.33	2.628	0.91
Switzerland	−9.395 (4.743)	1.248 (10.600)	−31.639 (19.455)	−0.004 (0.023)	0.13	1.242	0.65
Sweden	−24.531 (14.211)	15.589 (2.483)	−23.989 (6.455)	−0.029 (0.016)	0.79	0.820	0.79
Netherlands	−3.243 (11.409)	10.232 (3.244)	−16.121 (20.530)	−0.014 (0.038)	0.39	1.91	0.48
Belgium	−38.562 (10.281)	22.229 (4.919)	18.496 (11.193)	−0.008 (0.018)	0.78	0.941	0.74

Note: Figures in parentheses are standard errors. Constant terms were estimated in all equations.

the same time, it is encouraging to note that the coefficients on all variables (except the government-spending variable) are generally of the expected sign, although not always statistically significant.

To check the sensitivity of the analysis to model specification and different measures of inflationary expectations, the country equations were also estimated in the nominal interest form. Although the nominal equations generally provide a very similar picture to the real ones, it is interesting to note that, using all the different measures of inflationary expectations, the individual country coefficient estimates on expectations invariably provided little or no support for the Fisher hypothesis. This is despite the fact that the inflation coefficient was always close to unity in the aggregate model, supporting the Merrick and Saunders (1986) argument that aggregation may improve the power of tests involving expectations.

The evidence presented above supports the argument that capital mobility is high enough to make closed economy models suspect when tests on financial markets are being carried out. The evidence, however, is only circumstantial. It might be argued that the improved results from the 'world' model arise because the country equations are misspecified (perhaps due to random institutional reasons) and these specification errors tend to cancel in the aggregate.

To bring some more concrete evidence to bear on the capital mobility issue, one final set of estimations was carried out which tried to measure the importance of foreign policy variables on domestic interest rates. This was done by regressing each of the individual country interest rates on the 'world' policy variables.[15] If the improvement in the 'world' interest-rate equation is spurious, then the results of this final estimation should be no better than the individual equation results in Table 5.4. If, however, the improvement in the 'world' equation was due to the importance of capital-market integration, then the country interest rates regressed on aggregate policy variables should show some improvement over the country equations based only on closed economy assumptions.[16]

Table 5.5 presents the results for each country's interest-rate equation using 'world' policy explanatory variables. Apart from Switzerland, where no version of the model provides significant explanatory power,[17] there is generally as much variance explained by the 'world' variables as by the domestic policy variables, if not more. The cases of West Germany and Japan are the major exceptions, where the world variables do not explain as much as the domestic ones.[18] Encouragingly, the signs on the 'world' debt variables are all now positive and significant, while those on the money variable are all negative and significant; it appears, from these results, that real interest rates in both small and large economies are affected to a large degree (and with the correct signs) by the aggregated public financing decisions taken throughout the industrial world.

Before moving to the next chapter, it is worth spelling out clearly some of the limitations of the above analysis. It is true that the results point to problems, of misspecification bias for closed-economy-based Ricardian tests. However, it is also true that widely differing structural coefficients across countries may have introduced aggregation bias into the results for the 'world' model. Similarly, data limitations, particularly for Japan and Switzerland, reduce the force of any conclusions drawn. Some of these limitations may be overcome in the following chapter, which allows for asymmetries between the United States and non-US countries and uses more reliable data from the floating-rate period.

Table 5.5 'World' policy variables

Country	Estimated coefficients				Statistics		
	m	b	g	op	$\bar{R}^2$	SE	DW
United States	−70.273 (10.439)	24.168 (3.846)	−18.756 (22.701)	−0.058 (0.018)	0.87	0.915	0.966
West Germany	−29.556 (8.097)	11.527 (2.983)	−49.748 (17.607)	−0.013 (0.014)	0.46	0.710	1.16
Japan	−58.053 (35.861)	40.762 (13.211)	−43.618 (77.985)	−0.085 (0.061)	0.52	3.143	0.54
France	−72.191 (9.548)	19.024 (3.518)	−61.103 (20.765)	−0.028 (0.016)	0.82	0.837	1.74
United Kingdom	−48.977 (14.503)	29.324 (5.343)	−90.966 (31.541)	−0.062 (0.025)	0.78	1.271	1.18
Italy	−60.424 (23.062)	22.783 (8.496)	−84.290 (50.152)	−0.117 (0.039)	0.63	2.201	0.96
Canada	−53.171 (10.524)	24.286 (3.877)	−48.623 (22.886)	−0.036 (0.018)	0.82	0.922	1.22
Australia	−70.543 (15.897)	36.117 (5.857)	−51.256 (34.570)	−0.047 (0.027)	0.81	1.393	0.75
Switzerland	−14.495 (15.051)	7.045 (5.545)	−3.943 (32.732)	−0.002 (0.026)	0.02	1.319	0.65
Sweden	−50.936 (8.787)	20.602 (3.234)	−51.148 (19.109)	−0.026 (0.015)	0.82	0.770	1.23
Netherlands	−37.730 (19.415)	22.890 (7.153)	−0.960 (42.221)	−0.017 (0.033)	0.52	1.701	0.52
Belgium	−56.496 (11.560)	13.741 (4.259)	43.375 (25.140)	−0.011 (0.020)	0.74	1.013	0.85

Note: Figures in parentheses are standard errors. Constant terms were estimated in all equations.

Notes

1. There are still debates over just how mobile international capital really is. The work of Feldstein and Horioka (1980) has pointed towards rather limited mobility of capital, although more recent evidence by Frankel (1985) and Obstfeld (1986) has questioned this analysis.
2. See Blanchard (1985); Sachs and Wyplosz (1984) apply it in an income-expenditure model similar to the one above.
3. The portfolio balance model is generally presented in nominal terms, with the nominal rates of return entering the demand functions. As in other real models, it is necessary to omit inflationary expectations as an argument in the asset demand functions.
4. This is especially true for studies done using US data, where it is often argued that the US economy is large enough (or closed enough) to be modelled as a closed economy.

5. This equation is best described as a stripped down reduced form as many of the studies discussed in Chapter 4, use complex models containing many more domestic variables.

6. For a discussion of the importance of aggregation bias see Theil (1961). The work of Evans (1987b) provides some support for the assumption of equal cross-country coefficients.

7. In referring to the Fisher identity we do not include Fisher's hypothesis about the long-term constancy of the real interest rate.

8. See, for example, Feldstein (1986b) and Hoelscher (1986) where coefficients on the expected rate of inflation in long-term bond-rate equations were below unity. The main explanation for this in both cases was the problems in measuring inflationary expectations. The coefficient on expected inflation may also be less than one for theoretical reasons. In Makin (1983) a 'Mundell' effect is introduced into the LM equation so that higher inflationary expectations directly lower money demand and reduce the size of the Fisher effect. Makin's empirical results, however, do not confirm the presence of the so called 'Mundell' effect and it is not introduced in our model. In contrast, the presence of taxation on interest receipts may produce a coefficient on expected inflation that is greater than one, as in Feldstein (1986b). Hansson and Stuart (1986) show, in the open economy framework, that taking all of these factors into account should produce a unit coefficient on expected inflation.

9. Data for the OPEC current account were only available from 1970 onwards and have been set to zero from 1960 to 1969.

10. Central bank holdings of government debt are subtracted from the published total outstanding debt figures. For the United States, the foreign exchange reserves of the other countries were also subtracted from the total debt stock, under the assumption that non-US countries hold primarily US dollar government debt in their reserves.

11. Trend GNP is the antilogarithm of the fitted values from a regression of a constant and time on the logarithm of GNP.

12. The use of distributed lag proxies of expectations was very common in the early interest-rate literature such as Sargent (1969) and Feldstein and Eckstein (1970). However, even recent studies, such as Feldstein (1986b), have employed backward-looking measures of expectations. The rise in popularity of rational expectations models has led to the increasing use of forward measures of expectations, in particular, the use of actual *ex post* data. Fully rational expectations estimation is clearly not feasible (due to degrees-of-freedom limitations) in this study as long-run interest rates are used. The mixed approach is a recent innovation employed by Sachs (1985).

13. It is just significantly different from one at conventional levels.

14. The R^2 statistics are not reliable indicators in the second and third equations because they were estimated using two-stage least squares.

15. This is the same approach as employed by Evans (1987b), except that he imposes equal coefficients across countries.

16. These equations will still suffer from missing variables bias because they do not contain foreign interest-rate or exchange-rate expectation terms.

17. Discussions at the Swiss National Bank suggested data problems may be at the source of the weak Swiss results.

18. The Japanese equations explain very little of the variance in Japanese real rates. The same is true for the Swiss. This again may be due to data problems. (see Appendix A).

Chapter 6

A two-country model

Introduction

By focusing on 'world' debt, the previous chapter made it possible to explore issues of crowding-out at the 'world' level. The aggregative approach simplified the econometric analysis substantially, but was unable to throw any light on issues of transmission, exchange-rate determination, and the role of capital flows (or the current account) in the dynamics of adjustment. It is these latter issues that have captured the attention of national and international policy-makers during the 1980s. In particular, the massive appreciation of the US dollar (and subsequent depreciation), along with the associated current account imbalances, have led to growing calls for greater international policy co-ordination. In response, the G7 members have introduced what appears to be an informal system of exchange-rate targeting, and, at least through most of 1987, have been successful at keeping the US dollar within a narrow trading range. They have also raised the importance of co-ordinated policy decision-making, as reflected in a number of G7 summit meetings.

One of the key thrusts of these agreements has been for greater co-ordination of fiscal policy.[1] The United States has been asked (and has promised) to try and cut back on deficit financing, in return for increasing fiscal stimulus from Japan and West Germany. Such a policy package implies a very simple, symmetric theoretical framework, one that may not be realistic. The aim of this chapter is to set up a more general econometric model that can be used to explore the importance of deficit financing and the appropriateness of a symmetric analysis in the process of co-ordinated fiscal policy formation. The idea is to allow the data to determine whether or not the effects of US fiscal policy are symmetric to similar policies in the non-US bloc.

The chapter commences by outlining a theoretical model that is general enough to capture most of the recent innovations in the literature discussed in Chapters 2 and 3. Because it is relatively large, the model cannot be solved analytically and it is therefore estimated and solved numerically. The data base employed for estimation is then described. The problems involved with model estimation are then discussed, along with the results obtained. Finally, a numerical simulation technique is used to solve the model and to evaluate its dynamic properties. The response of the model to exogenous increases in government debt, in both the United States and non-US bloc, is also analysed. Some in-sample simulations are also used to undertake historical policy evaluation. The final section concludes by pointing out the limitations of the work and suggesting areas for further development.

The main conclusions from the chapter are that the wealth and port-folio effects of debt have an important impact on international financial markets, in particular, on current account imbalances and the dynamics of real exchange-rate adjustment. These effects are not symmetric, suggesting that government bonds issued by different countries have different risk characteristics (this may originate from both political and exchange-rate risk).[2] The conclusions have important implications for policy co-ordination that will be explored further in Chapter 7.

The theory

A general framework

In specifying a two-country model, one aim was to keep the framework as simple as possible so that results could be easily interpreted. At the same time, it was necessary to allow for enough structure to test the hypotheses raised in Chapters 2 and 3, and to enable the model to track the sample data. Given these conflicting aims, there were inevitably compromises to be made. Unlike in Chapter 5, where it was possible to write down a theoretical proposition and then test it with one pass through the data, a multi-country model must be built by trial and error. It rarely happens that it is possible to estimate a large system of equations and then solve it on the first round, giving sensible paths for all endogenous variables. Rather, it is usually necessary to examine the first round solution, isolate problem variables and respecify entire sections of the theory, then re-estimate, re-solve and so on . . . The other alternative is to stick with the original model but to adjust the dynamic solution by changing parameters or using the infamous 'add factors'. This second alternative may be justified when the primary purpose of the model is forecasting, but when the model is to be used for hypothesis testing, there is little point in adopting this approach: it is then no longer possible to determine what results reflect the underlying theory and data, and what results reflect the *ad hoc* adjustments.

To be consistent with the iterative way in which the research was conducted, this section starts with the most general model that was estimated and relates it to the theoretical literature discussed in Chapters 2 and 3. The following subsection then discusses the final specification used in the estimation and solution of the model. In justifying the final specification it is necessary to discuss the solution paths for alternative specifications of the model which may have been rejected on the grounds of poor estimation results or model instability.

The model, in its most general form, is set out in equations (6.1) to (6.12) (All notation is explained in Table 6.1). For each domestic equation there is a symmetric foreign country equation, not listed, except for those equations relating to bilateral variables (exchange rates and so on). The model encompasses, as special cases, much of the recent work on real exchange rates (and could be extended to cover nominal exchange-rate models). It is a two-country model in which each country produces a domestic non-traded good, as well as an internationally traded good. Each country also issues a domestic non-traded asset, as well as an internationally traded asset. The real exchange rate is determined, therefore, both in the asset markets, along the lines of Branson *et al.* (1977), and in the goods market, as derived in the early Mundell–Fleming framework and as is still used in many of the real intertemporal models.

$$h_d(P_h, P_x, a) + g_h = 0 \tag{6.1}$$

$$x_d(P_h, P_x, a) + x_d^*(P_h^*, P_x, a^*) + g_x + g_x^* = 0 \tag{6.2}$$

$$a = f(w, \bar{y}_d, r) \tag{6.3}$$

$$w = m + b_s + nfa \tag{6.4}$$

$$y = a + g + x_d^* - eim_d \tag{6.5}$$

$$m_s - m_d(r, r^*, E\dot{e}, y)w = 0 \tag{6.6}$$

$$b_s - b_d(r, r^*, E\dot{e})w - eb_{d*}(r, r^*, E\dot{e})w^* = 0 \tag{6.7}$$

$$g = \tau + \dot{b} + \dot{m} - r\dot{e}s \tag{6.8}$$

$$ca = (x_d^* - eim_d) - rb_{d*} + er^*b_d^* \tag{6.9}$$

$$nfa = eb_d^* - b_{d*} = nfa_{(t-1)} + ca_{(t)} - r\dot{e}s_{(t)} \tag{6.10}$$

$$E\log\dot{e} = \theta(E\log\bar{e} - \log e) \tag{6.11}$$

$$\log\bar{e} = \alpha^*\log P_h^* - \alpha\log P_h + (\beta^* - \beta)\log P_x \tag{6.12}$$

Table 6.1 List of notation

P_h/P_H	= real/nominal price of home good
P_x/P_X	= real/nominal price of export good
P_i/P_I	= real/nominal price of import good
a	= private absorption
y	= real output
$\bar{y}_d$	= lifetime disposable income
w	= real wealth in terms of domestically produced goods
r	= real interest rate
e	= real exchange rate (a rise in e represents a depreciation)
e_N	= nominal exchange rate
τ	= real taxes
nfa	= net foreign assets
ca	= current account
m	= real money in terms of domestically produced goods
b	= real bonds in terms of domestically produced goods
g	= government spending on goods
res	= central bank reserves
h	= non-traded or home good
x	= home country's export good
im	= home country's import (foreign country's export) good
E	= forward expectations operator
P_C	= nominal consumer price index
α	= share of home goods in consumption
β	= share of export goods in consumption
θ	= speed-of-adjustment parameter

Note: Capital letters refer to nominal variables and small letters refer to real variables. Stars refer to foreign variables, dots represent time derivatives and a bar over a variable indicates its long-run steady-state level. The subscript d denotes demand for a variable (excess demand in the case of the goods market) and the subscript s denotes exogenously given supply of a variable.

The inclusion of traded bonds that are imperfect substitutes is not common to most of the small multi-country models such as MINIMOD or the Knight and Masson (1985) model. This extension, although complicating the model substantially, was considered to be crucial to examining the exchange-rate effects of government debt. The additional complication of having goods that are imperfect substitutes was included, not because this is crucial for testing hypotheses about debt, but because the versions of the model estimated without this extension were not able to track historical data well; they did, however, produce qualitatively similar simulation results.

Equations (6.1) and (6.2) represent the market-clearing conditions for the four goods in the model. The home good is assumed to be labour services, so that P_h is in fact a measure of real wages. This is a common assumption in the non-traded goods literature (see, for example, Eichengreen and Wyplosz 1986; Frenkel and Razin 1987). It can be justified on the grounds that labour mobility is still highly restricted in nearly all the major industrial economies. All goods prices are expressed in units of the imported good. The export and import goods are produced only in the home and foreign economies respectively, leaving three relative goods prices in the model. The excess demand functions are similar to, but simplified versions of, those discused in Katseli (1983). These market-clearing conditions could easily be replaced by *ad hoc* price-adjustment rules, as is common in much of the neo-Keynesian macro-literature.

Equation (6.3) is the same absorption function as used in Chapter 5. It expresses total absorption as a positive function of financial wealth and expected lifetime income[3] and a negative function of the real interest rate. This is similar to the Sachs and Wyplosz (1984) specification and can be derived from an intertemporal framework where Ricardian equivalence does not fully hold (as in Blanchard 1985). Note that, because government debt is included in wealth, an increase in debt has a direct impact on private absorption. The coefficient on wealth will, of course, depend on how important any future tax discounting is to consumers.

Equation (6.4) is a standard definition of wealth. It is the sum of money, domestic bonds and net foreign assets. It differs from the definition used in the empirical work of Chapter 5 because of the inclusion of net foreign assets. It will be recalled that bilateral net foreign asset positions dropped out of the analysis after aggregation. In contrast, the use of the two-country model now implies important feedback from fiscal shocks to the other country's wealth position. This interdependence will be a major feature driving the dynamics of the model. The exclusion of real capital from the multi-country model was felt to be a reasonable simplification given the addition of the extra dynamic provided through the current account and net foreign asset adjustment. Some discussion of the possible role of capital accumulation will still be possible by drawing on the estimated coefficients from the 'world' economy model presented in Appendix B. This approach can also be justified by the fact that the reduced-form coefficients on debt in the world interest-rate equations are not greatly affected by the inclusion of the capital stock variable (see Appendix B).

The national income identity is presented in equation (6.5). This is standard and is similar to the income identity used in Chapter 5. It could also be written simply as the sum of the production of the home and export good.

Equations (6.6) and (6.7) represent the demand for real money and bonds in the portfolio balance framework. Asset demands are a function of all rates of return, wealth and portfolio preferences. Money is the only asset used for transaction purposes, so is a positive function of income. The supply of bonds must equal the sum of both domestic and foreign demands for each of the traded assets, providing a completely symmetric analysis to the goods market. This same asset market framework, in an *n*-country setting, was employed in Chapter 5 to highlight the importance of foreign variables for domestic interest-rate determination. In the 'world' aggregate model, imperfect substitutability was assumed away, leaving only equation (6.6) to derive a reduced form. The advantage of the multi-country model is that the addition of equation (6.7) alllows the explicit test of the previous assumption that government bonds are close substitutes.

Equation (6.8) is the same temporal government budget constraint as used in Chapter 5. It ensures that government expenditure is financed through taxes, deficits, printing money or running down reserves. The authorities have five policy variables, of which only four are linearly independent. As is done in much of the theoretical work, it is assumed that taxes adjust automatically to maintain a desired level of government debt (Barro 1974). Shocks to the level of government debt can then be considered as a helicopter drop, with the resulting change in taxes having no real effects. In other words, people realize that a one-period deficit will involve higher taxes to pay the interest on the debt, but they need not expect to repay the whole amount of the increase in debt during their lifetime. This assumption allows the model to highlight permanent wealth and portfolio effects of deficits, rather than the short-run income effects normally stressed in macroeconomic models.

Equation (6.9) is the dynamic adjustment mechanism for the current account; the sum of the trade balance and net interest payments. This equation provides the most important source of dynamics to the model by allowing each country to swap its assets for the other country's goods. In the long run, the current account will be balanced, ensuring both flow and stock equilibrium. Notice that the current account and therefore net foreign assets are written in domestic currency. There are, however, valuation effects in the determination of net foreign assets, as seen in equation (6.10). The importance of these will depend on the denomination of outstanding assets and liabilities. The equation defines the net foreign asset position as the sum of past current account imbalances, or simply as the difference between the two countries' holdings of each other's bonds.

The last two equations provide important definitions needed for the solution of the model. Equation (6.11) is the Dornbusch (1976) approach to explaining exchange-rate expectations formation.[4] It is based on a partial adjustment towards an expected long-run equilibrium exchange-rate. The long-run equilibrium exchange rate is, in turn, defined in equation (6.12) as a weighted sum of the three relative goods prices in the model, the weights being the consumption shares of the goods. The definition of the long-run real exchange rate as a vector of relative goods prices is one of the distinctive features of the model. It ensures that deviations from a simple purchasing power parity rule are (at least partially) an equilibrium phenomenon and may persist in the long run. Such a result is in sharp contrast to the Dornbusch (1976) type of monetary model, where purchasing power parity holds in the long run. Because the long-run real exchange rate is very important to the model, it is worth examining just where it comes from.

The definition of the long-run real exchange rate is derived as follows. Assume that the nominal consumer price level is a geometrically weighted (using consumption weights) average of the three domestically consumed goods. Then (in logs[5]) we get,

$$P_C = \alpha P_H + \beta P_X + (1 - \alpha - \beta) P_I \qquad (6.13)$$

$$P_C^\star = \alpha^\star P_H^\star + \beta^\star P_X^\star + (1 - \alpha^\star - \beta^\star) P_I^\star. \qquad (6.13a)$$

Subtracting (6.13) from (6.13a) gives

$$P_C^\star - P_C = \alpha^\star (P_H^\star - P_I^\star) - \alpha (P_H - P_I) + \beta^\star (P_X^\star - P_I^\star) - \beta (P_X - P_I) + P_I^\star - P_I. \qquad (6.14)$$

Assuming the law of one price holds for the same goods, that is,

$$P_I - P_I^\star = e_N, \qquad (6.15)$$

(where e_N is the nominal exchange rate), then we can write the equation in real terms as

$$P_C^\star - P_C + e_N = \alpha^\star P_h^\star - \alpha P_h + (\beta^\star - \beta) P_x, \qquad (6.16)$$

which is the definition of the steady-state real exchange rate in the models.

One of the main conclusions of Katseli (1983) was that a model containing the type of goods markets specified above will provide few unambiguous conclusions for the real exchange rate (even without much structure on the asset market side). It will be recalled that, even in the two-good models of Frenkel and Razin (1985; 1986a; 1986b), the effects of fiscal policy on the exchange rate generally depend on the relative size of the various consumption propensities across countries and across sectors.

Similar ambiguities arise within the class of real models that have substantial financial structure (but limited goods-market detail). In particular, models that contain imperfect substitution between domestic and foreign bonds inevitably can say little about the impact of long-run effects of deficits on the real exchange rate. This was seen in Chapter 3 in the discussion of Branson (1985), Sachs and Wyplosz (1984) and Kole (1985). The reason (first discussed by Branson *et al.* 1977) is that a fundamental source of ambiguity is in the asset markets. This can be shown clearly by normalizing the bond-market equilibrium condition, that is, equation (6.7), on exchange-rate expectations,[6]

$$\dot{Ee}_t = r_t - r_t^\star + Q(b_t^\star - b_t),\tag{6.17}$$

where Q, the risk premium, is a non-linear function of asset substitutability and capital mobility parameters. As shown by Kole (1985), the risk premium in a two-country model should in fact be a function of the outstanding bond stocks relative to each country's demand for the two assets (wealth). Such a formulation is both functionally difficult to handle, and almost impossible to implement empirically; data on asset holdings by currency are generally not available. The simplified form used above should still pick up the primary determinants of risk; it has also been used in other empirical studies (Frankel 1983; Dooley and Isard 1980).

Substituting equation (6.11) into equation (6.17) gives

$$e_t = \bar{e}_t + 1/\theta(r_t^\star - r_t) + Q/\theta(b_t - b_t^\star).\tag{6.18}$$

From equation (6.18) it is clear that government debt policy will impact on the current real exchange rate through three channels. The first channel is via the long-run relative goods prices in the model and will depend on all the parameters in the model; in particular, the relative propensities of governments to consume home versus foreign goods, the degree of substitutability in asset and goods markets and the initial level of asset-market integration. The second channel is more straightforward. As long as a budget deficit raises domestic real interest rates, then the impact effect of a deficit will be to appreciate the domestic currency. This is the standard channel that both Evans (1986) and Feldstein (1986a) appear to have been testing in their reduced-form empirical models.[7] It is, in fact, the only fiscal channel that survives once the above model is simplified down to the more common sticky price monetary model estimated by Frankel (1979) and Sachs (1985). The final, and most direct, channel for debt policy to impact on the real exchange rate is by increasing the stock of domestic bonds and the risks associated with holding those bonds. If bonds are not perfect substitutes, this effect will depreciate the currency on impact (relative to the long-run equilibrium) to ensure that, over time, there will be an appreciation of the real exchange rate. As stressed in Chapter 4, the overall effects (or reduced-form coefficient) of debt cannot be signed unambiguously. To ensure that the empirical model can distinguish between these alternative channels, equation (6.18) will be used below as the core of the multi-country model.

The empirical model

The above theoretical model is a highly non-linear simultaneous system of mostly dynamic equations. The model contains nine independent functional relationships and nine identities (including the foreign country equations) making a total of eighteen endogenous variables to be solved for. A solution to the system can only be obtained by assuming either fixed relative prices or fixed relative supplies of goods. In the empirical work that follows (the empirical model is constituted by equations (6.21) to (6.26) below), the emphasis is on relative price adjustment, so for estimation and simulation purposes real output is taken as given.

Given the highly non-linear and simultaneous nature of the theoretical model, it is likely that substantial gains in efficiency may be obtained by using a FIML estimation procedure of the entire model as it stands in equations (6.1) to (6.12). At this stage, however, each equation has been linearized and normalized on an endogenous variable (for reasons that will be discussed below). The normalization chosen was arbitrary, which would not matter if a full-system estimation procedure is used, but it may make a difference when single equation techniques are employed. There does not appear to be any theoretical technique available for deciding on the appropriate normalization, and it appears from the literature that common sense is the only guide available.

The goods-market equilibrium conditions were used to obtain equations for the relative goods prices. The absorption function was initially included in the empirical framework directly, but the coefficients on lagged absorption were so close to unity that this introduced instability into the model.[8] One response to this problem would have been to try and improve the model's stability by more detailed disaggregation and/or by adjusting the model's parameters. However, the response taken was in the other direction — absorption was substituted out of each equation — to keep the model as simple as possible. While the overall model simulates much better using this approach, a number of equations do perform worse without an absorption variable (this is particularly true of the current account equations).

As in Chapter 5, an exogenous oil sector was introduced into the model at the estimation stage. This was done to capture the effects of OPEC price changes on the relative goods prices in the models. A real oil price variable o, was included as an explanatory variable in each of the relative price equations. The sign of this coefficient should be negative, as a rise in oil prices reduces income available for spending on other goods in the model.

A final adjustment to the goods-market sector was the inclusion of a partial adjustment mechanism in the relative price equations. This was employed because the model is estimated using quarterly data and markets are unlikely to clear in such a time-span. Even more importantly, the law of one price is not likely to hold on a quarterly basis.[9] The law of one price assumption was crucial in deriving our definition of the real exchange rate and it is necessary to follow through the implications of slow adjustment in the pricing of each good to the rest of the model. One obvious point from this assumption is that each country may have different terms of trade (that is, a different relative export price), as the same export good may be priced differently in different markets. It is important to see formally how this changes the definition of the real exchange rate presented in equation (6.12).

As an example, assume that it takes two periods for the law of one price to hold; then (again in logs)

$$P_{I_t} = \theta(e_{N_t} - P_{I_t}^{\star}) + (1 - \theta)(e_{N_{t-1}} - P_{I_{t-1}}^{\star}), \tag{6.19}$$

where θ is an adjustment parameter between zero and unity. If equation (6.19) is used instead of equation (6.15) to derive a definition of the real exchange rate, then the result is

$$e_t = \alpha^{\star} P_{h_t}^{\star} - \alpha P_{h_t} + \beta^{\star} P_{x_t}^{\star} - \beta P_{x_t} + (\theta - 1)(e_{N_t} + P_{I_t}) + (1 - \theta)(e_{N_{t-1}} + P_{I_{t-1}}). \tag{6.20}$$

The definition of the short-run real exchange rate in equation (6.20) differs from the steady-state exchange rate in equation (6.12). There are now two terms-of-trade variables and both a current and lagged nominal exchange-rate disturbance.[10] In the steady state, the definition given in equation (6.20) will be identical to that in equation (6.12). In this case, when

$$e_{N_{t-1}} - P_{I_{t-1}}^{\star} = e_{N_t} - P_{I_t}^{\star},$$

then the last two terms in equation (6.20) cancel and $P_x^{\star}$ will equal P_x.

At any point in time, the real exchange rate in financial markets can jump to assure that asset markets clear; this is not true for the relative goods prices which adjust only slowly towards their steady-state path. This is a key feature of the model and will be used, via expectations formation, to link the financial and real sectors in the adjustment from short- to long-run equilibrium. The final relative price equations are given by equations (6.21) and (6.22).[11]

$$P_{h_t} = \gamma_0 + \gamma_1 P_{x_t} + \gamma_2 w_t - \gamma_3 r_t + \gamma_4 g_t - \gamma_5 o_t + \gamma_6 P_{h_{t-1}}, \tag{6.21}$$

$$P_{x_t} = \delta_0 + \delta_1 P_{h_t} + \delta_2 P_{x_t}^{\star} + \delta_3 w_t - \delta_4 r_t + \delta_5 g_t - \delta_6 o_t + \delta_7 P_{x_{t-1}}. \tag{6.22}$$

Coefficients that are unambiguously negative are marked as such. Many of the coefficients with a positive sign cannot be signed unambiguously and may also turn out to be negative at the estimation stage[12]

The money demand equations

$$r_t = \xi_0 - \xi_1 m_t + \xi_2 w_t + \xi_3 g_t + \xi_4 r_t^\star + \xi_5 E\dot{e}_t + \xi_6 r_{t-1} \tag{6.23}$$

were normalized on the real rate of interest in each bloc producing interest-rate equations that are very similar to those derived in Chapter 5. Real income is again substituted out. To separate the wealth and portfolio effects of money (which have opposite signs) the wealth variable was not disaggregated. The main innovation in the interest-rate equations is the explicit inclusion of international linkages, via the foreign interest-rate term and the exchange-rate expectations term. The model includes directly the interrelationship between interest and exchange rates. It is therefore well equipped to pick up the joint response of these two variables to fiscal shocks. A lagged interest-rate term is included in the equations, again following problems of model instability. Given that asset markets are supposed to adjust instantly, the lagged endogenous variable can only be justified on the grounds of an adaptive expectations mechanism, whereby expected future changes to the exogenous variables are a function of past changes in exogenous variables. This is an area that requires further investigation.

The real exchange-rate equation,

$$e_t = \eta_0 + \eta_1 P_{h_t}^\star - \eta_2 P_{h_t} + \eta_3 P_{x_t}^\star - \eta_4 P_{x_t} + \eta_5(r_t^\star - r_t) + \eta_6 b_t - \eta_7 b_t^\star, \tag{6.24}$$

has already been derived above. The only alteration is that the expected steady-state exchange rate $E\bar{e}$ has been replaced by the vector of actual observed relative goods prices

$$E\bar{e}_t = \alpha^\star P_{h_t}^\star - \alpha P_{h_t} + \beta^\star P_{x_t}^\star - \beta P_{x_t}. \tag{6.25}$$

This provides the anchor for the current real exchange rate. A similar real exchange-rate equation, but without the financial market detail, has been derived by Barro (1983). As far as I know, the above model is the first explicitly to include imperfect substitution in both goods and asset markets in the exchange-rate equation.

The other variables in the equation — the interest differential and the bond stocks — force the current exchange rate to deviate from its expected steady-state level in a way that is consistent with the required change in the exchange rate over time. The required rate of change in the exchange rate, in turn, is such that holders of bonds are satisfied with the relative rates of return on their portfolio. Consistency is ensured by including the same measure of exchange-rate expectations in the interest-rate equations as is used in the derivation of exchange-rate equation.[13]

With estimated equation for the current account,

$$ca_t = \omega_0 + \sum_{i=0}^{9} \omega_i e_{t-i} - \omega_{10}\omega_t + \omega_{11}\omega_t^\star - \omega_{12}g_t + \omega_{13}g_t^\star + \omega_{14}nfa_{t-1}$$
$$- \omega_{15}o_t + \omega_{16}ca_{t-1}, \tag{6.26}$$

the empirical model is complete. Because absorption was again substituted out, and because the current account equation is a linearized version of a non-linear function, there were a number of problems encountered in estimation and simulation of this sector. There appeared to be multicollinearity between a number of variables. The main problem variables were the real interest rates. These should be included because of their effects on both interest payments and on absorption. However, the inclusion of the interest rates seemed to change the dynamics of the model in an unstable way, and they have been dropped from the final version.[14] The remaining variables have standard interpretations. The equation contains a distributed lag on the real exchange rate to allow for 'J curve' effects. Domestic wealth and government spending have positive effects on absorption and a negative impact on the current account, as long as restrictions are placed on relative consumption parameters. In contrast, higher net foreign assets raise interest earnings and improve the current account. Finally, a lagged current account term is included to allow for slow adjustment in trade flows.

A stable steady-state solution to the model depends on a balanced current account in the long run. The current account equations are therefore important for the model's solution, even although the current account is not the primary focus of attention in the book. The so called 'Super Marshall Lerner Condition', as discussed by Branson (1985), requires that the positive effects of a surplus in the current account on interest payments (via higher net foreign assets) are more than offset by the negative effects of the surplus on the trade account (generated by higher wealth and an appreciation of the exchange rate).

The data

It was initially hoped to estimate the model using the same data base as was used in the 'world' aggregate model, that is, annual data for twelve countries from 1960 to 1985. A number of constraints arose during data collection and estimation making this approach unfeasible. The most obvious constraint was on data availability. For a number of countries, the extra data required were just not available, particularly in the early years. For this reason, and also to reduce the size of the data-collection and data-manipulation tasks, it was decided to reduce the rest-of-the-world bloc to the non-US G7 members. It was then possible to estimate an annual version of the two-country model. However, despite reasonable coefficient estimates, this version did not have a stable solution. One possible reason for the lack of success at simulating the annual model may be due to the regime change that occurred in the switch from fixed to flexible exchange rates. The process of expectations formation may have altered following this switch, as may have many of the structural coefficients.[15]. There is also the problem of degrees of freedom, which were very limited for a number of equations. The final model estimation reported below is therefore based on quarterly data over the period 1973:2 to 1985:4.

A full description of the data source is provided in Appendix A. Many of the data are identical to those used in Chapter 5, except that they are sampled quarterly. Variables not discussed in Chapter 5 include: the real exchange rate, — the nominal exchange rate times the ratio of foreign to domestic consumer prices,[16] the real price of home goods, P_h — proxied by the domestic wage rate and deflated by an average of export and import unit values; the terms of trade for each country are the ratio of export and import unit values; the real price of oil, o — the spot price for Saudi Arabian crude, deflated by the US consumer price index; the current account, ca — taken directly from the IFS (in billions of US dollars); and finally, the net foreign asset position of each country, nfa — calculated by cumulating current accounts.[17]

The aggregation technique for the non-US bloc was again varied to check for the sensitivity of the results. As in Chapter 5, the type of weights made little difference to the general results obtained. The use of variable weights was avoided as this would have required the inclusion of an endogenous variable (the exchange rate) in the construction of other explanatory variables. In fact, estimations and simulations using variable weights produced very similar results to those reported. It was also decided not to use differing weights for different variables to avoid excessive complications. The final weights employed were based on average shares in world GNP over the entire floating-rate period. In other multi-country models exchange rates are often aggregated using trade weights or with weights derived from a country's role in international financial markets. In a model where the exchange rate is determined by the interaction of goods and financial markets, it is not clear whether either of these approaches is superior, and, apart from the case of Canada, it does not appear that widely different weights should result from using them.[18]

Model estimation

Estimation issues

As with most of the recent multi-country models, the estimation has not been carried out using a FIML procedure. Despite the obvious gains in efficiency that may be obtained from using FIML, the disadvantages are also great. This is particularly so for a small or medium-sized special-purpose model, where the specification of many sectors was deliberately kept to a minimum of detail. In this case, with some equations obviously misspecified, a FIML technique would infect the estimation of the whole system with misspecification bias, rather than keeping it within known sectors. The other limitation of employing a FIML estimation technique is the additional computational burden involved, for what may be only a limited gain in overall efficiency. Two-stage least squares has therefore been applied to equations (6.21) to (6.26), with instruments employed including all exogenous variables and a subset of relevant lagged endogenous variables.

A major issue in all models of financial markets is how to handle expected future variables. Traditionally, the estimation of multi-country models has involved a wide range of approaches to finding proxies for unobservable expectations. The most common has been the use of an adaptive expectations assumption, allowing distributed lags to be employed as proxies for forward-looking expectations. More recently, there has been an attempt to introduce rational expectations into the area of multi-country modelling. To date there are still very few cases of multi-country models that are estimated under the assumption of rationality across all sectors, although there are a number of models which employ rational expectations as a means of solving a system estimated with single-equation procedures.

The approach taken in this book has been to avoid the use of the rational expectations assumption in the model estimation for a number of reasons. First, there is growing evidence that the rationality assumption (as implemented empirically) may not be a reasonable approximation of the real world (see Frankel and Froot 1987). Second, the rationality assumption implies strong cross-equation restrictions on the model which should be tested using a FIML estimation procedure, something already rejected above. Third, it is unlikely that a rational expectations solution and simulation programme could have been developed for the model, given the computing and time constraints faced. Finally, the additional insights to be gained by using rational expectations do not appear to be great. This is particularly true if the exchange rate is allowed to jump (as in the approach used); the same general results should obtain for the impact and dynamic effects of debt on exchange rates under both static and rational expectations, as was shown by Knight and Masson (1985). The major difference being that there should be more overshooting under the static rather than the rational expectations assumption.

Estimation results

The estimation results reported below are only one of many estimated versions of the model. As stressed above, a number of differing specifications have been estimated and simulated. No attempt will be made to discuss all the versions of the model or even all those that produced sensible simulation results. It is true, however, that the general conclusions from both estimation and simulation are not widely different for the other versions of the model. This is particularly so for the effects of government debt in the system; the coefficients on debt variables were both stable and generally significant in all versions estimated.

Table 6.2 provides the estimated coefficients, along with Durbin–Watson statistics and the standard errors of the equations.[19] The R^2 statistics are not reported as the fit of the individual equations is not relevant for model-building purposes. In fact, they were all reasonably high — around 0.90 — including the real exchange-rate equation. Plots of actual against fitted values were also very encouraging. The exchange-rate equation performed particularly well relative to most recent single-equation models. The poor tracking ability of standard models is fully discussed by Meese and Rogoff (1983a; 1983b; 1985). It should be pointed out, however, that the sort of analysis undertaken by Meese and Rogoff is not particularly useful when the exchange-rate equation contains other endogenous variables. The tracking ability of the exchange-rate equation then depends on simultaneous interactions of all endogenous variables and can only be evaluated using simultaneous equation solutions, something not done by Meese and Rogoff.

Looking first at the goods market (that is, the relative price equations), it is clear that few generalizations can be made about coefficients, either across sectors or across countries. This was to be expected, given that many of the coefficients in these equations could not be signed unambiguously, but depend on relative consumption propensities across countries and sectors. The speed-of-adjustment parameters indicate fairly fast adjustment of goods prices towards their equilibrium level. The coefficients on the oil-price variable are all negative as expected. An interesting point to note is that the oil coefficient in the home goods price equation for the non-US bloc is double that in the US equation. This was to be expected given the greater dependence of the non-US countries on imported oil. It has important implications for the long-run real exchange

Table 6.2 Empirical results

Variables	Coefficients											SE	DW
P_{h_t}	P_{x_t} −0.207 (0.172)	ω_t 1.300 (0.461)	r_t −.022 (0.008)	g_t 0.112 (0.738)	o_t −0.076 (0.030)	$P_{h_{t-1}}$ 0.664 (0.177)						0.026	0.84
$P_{h_t}^\star$	$P_{x_t}^\star$ 0.014 (0.096)	$\omega_t^\star$ 0.504 (0.281)	$r_t^\star$ 0.007 (0.001)	$g_t^\star$ −0.097 (0.840)	o_t −0.031 (0.020)	$P_{h_{t-1}}^\star$ 0.618 (0.084)						0.017	0.55
P_{x_t}	P_{h_t} 0.396 (0.092)	$P_{h_t}^\star$ −0.170 (0.085)	ω_t −0.783 (0.285)	r_t −0.000 (0.006)	g_t −0.392 (0.521)	o_t −0.045 (0.021)	$P_{x_{t-1}}$ 0.617 (0.055)					0.016	1.16
$P_{x_t}^\star$	$P_{h_t}^\star$ −0.087 (0.149)	P_{x_t} 0.139 (0.143)	$\omega_t^\star$ 0.871 (0.370)	$r_t^\star$ 0.004 (0.003)	$g_t^\star$ 0.660 (1.085)	o_t −0.043 (0.032)	$P_{x_{t-1}}^\star$ 0.552 (0.102)					0.023	1.22
r_t	m_t 0.346 (11.968)	g_t −13.068 (11.769)	o_t 0.629 (0.351)	$r_t^\star$ 0.102 (0.066)	$E\dot{e}_t$ 3.382 (2.440)	r_{t-1} 0.714 (0.073)						0.330	1.53
$r_t^\star$	$m_t^\star$ −0.538 (19.493)	$g_t^\star$ 27.357 (11.324)	$g_t^\star$ 6.615 (31.271)	o_t 0.264 (0.595)	r_t 0.281 (0.131)	$E\dot{e}_t$ −5.842 (3.020)	$r_{t-1}^\star$ 0.619 (0.131)					0.582	1.45
e_t	P_{h_t} 0.388 (0.187)	$P_{h_t}^\star$ −1.405 (0.147)	$P_{x_t}^\star$ 0.378 (0.190)	P_{x_t} −0.022 (0.190)	$(r_t^\star - r_t)$ 0.026 (0.005)	b_t 1.372 (0.244)	$b_t^\star$ 1.996 (0.480)					0.031	1.75
ca_t	e_t −26.156 (10.381)	e_{t-3} 16.376 (10.801)	e_{t-6} 18.410 (17.430)	e_{t-9} 21.776 (17.584)	ω_t 29.148 (34.960)	ω_t −29.061 (75.170)	g_t −1.726 (243.13)	$g_t^\star$ 110.99 (221.11)	nfa_{t-1} −327.78 (143.11)	o_t 2.948 (3.401)	ca_{t-1} 0.549 (0.188)	3.058	2.54
$ca_t^\star$	e_t 5.056 (7.115)	e_{t-3} −1.911 (9.791)	e_{t-6} 2.901 (10.920)	e_{t-9} −17.629 (11.647)	ω_t −18.365 (41.225)	$\omega_t^\star$ −199.22 (65.263)	g_t 85.328 (140.89)	$g_t^\star$ −11.804 (175.31)	$nfa_{t-1}^\star$ 96.890 (95.81)	o_t −8.487 (2.833)	$ca_{t-1}^\star$ 0.611 (0.123)	2.408	2.32

Notes: Standard errors are in parentheses. Constant terms were estimated in all equations. All equations were estimated using two-stage least squares.

rate; a one percentage-point rise in the real price of oil would appreciate the real US dollar by around 3 per cent if one looks only at the direct goods market effects.[20]

Of the other coefficients, less than half were significant. No attempt was made to respecify these equations or to drop those variables that were insignificant as they were not the primary area of interest and the quarterly volatility and likely measurement error may help explain the low significance of the coefficients.[21] The Durbin–Watson statistics point towards problems of serial correlation in these equations. No correction was made for this because there are already lagged endogenous variables in the specification and there are no theoretical reasons for serial correlation to be present in the model. The serial correlation seems likely to be the result of the partial specification, that is, from missing variables.[22]

The real interest-rate equations, particularly the non-US equation, also have a large number of insignificant coefficients. This was partly a result of including the lagged adjustment term, which was done to improve the overall model performance. The most important variables, for simulation purposes, are the wealth terms; they have the right sign and are significant at the 95 per cent level. Also important for the model's dynamics are the interest-rate and exchange-rate expectations terms. These have the right sign in both equations, although they are insignificant in the non-US bloc. There was again no attempt made to drop insignificant or incorrectly signed variables; in any case they were generally not important variables for simulation purposes.

The real exchange-rate equation is the most important equation linking both the two-country blocs and the two sectors in the country together. A number of different specifications of this equation were tried with the aim of developing a complete structural equation in which financial markets dominated short-term exchange-rate movements but goods markets determined the steady-state level of the exchange rate. In general, the final equation presented in Table 6.2 compares very well with the recent single-equation literature. The standard error of the equation, at 3.1 per cent, is very low and the Durbin–Watson statistic is reasonable at 1.75. Of the differing specifications (corresponding to many of the traditional exchange-rate models) for this equation that have been examined, none provided anything near as good a fit or as sensible coefficient estimates.[23] However, as mentioned above, the real test of the equation must be done using a full model simulation.

Looking more closely at the coefficients, it can be seen that the relative goods prices are all correctly signed, and only that for US terms of trade is insignificant; this suggests that there are significant equilibrium deviations from purchasing power parity. The real interest differential is correctly signed and the most significant variable in the equation. The risk-premium determinants — the two bond-stock variables — are both significant but the coefficient on the US bond stock has an unexpected sign. The equation implies that an increase in the stock of government bonds in the non-US bloc adds a risk premium to holding those bonds and depreciates the exchange rate (relative to the expected long-run rate). In contrast, the reverse happens for an increase in the stock of US bonds, implying that the private sector in both countries does not mind expanding the share of US assets in their portfolios.[24]

Explaining why an increase in US bonds actually appreciates the US dollar is not easy. The only reason why the exchange rate appreciates following a fiscal expansion is that domestic interest rates rise, or because of direct effects on relative goods prices. As these effects are already included in the equation, the coefficient on US debt should either be zero or negative, not positive. Feldstein (1986a), who also finds this result, has argued that US debt must effect the expected long-run rate directly via some channel not yet thought of. It is perhaps more likely that this paradox emerges because of measurement error in real interest rates, or multicollinearity.[25]

The final estimations for the current account are important for analysing the dynamic effects of debt. To avoid serious multicollinearity problems a number of the lagged exchange-rate terms were dropped from the estimation. The final lag structure shows a typical 'J-curve' effect of the exchange rate on the current account, with the adverse impact effect being particularly strong for the non-US bloc. The wealth and government spending coefficients are included to represent absorption effects. These cannot be signed unambiguously and many are insignificant, although they do not seem to cause problems for the model as a whole. In contrast, the wrong sign on the non-US net foreign asset variable does lead to some instabilities in the model simulation. These problems of model simulation are discussed in the next section.

To summarize briefly, the final estimation of the model provides very strong support for a structural exchange-rate equation allowing for permanent deviations from both purchasing power parity and interest parity. The heavy use of these simplifying parity conditions, in so much of the previous empirical work on exchange rates, may explain the lack of recent success in exchange-rate modelling. The other estimated equations in the model are not as robust. They show signs of serial correlation in the errors, pointing to problems of incomplete specification; further work on these equations is certainly called for. Full evaluation of the model should not be based only on the single equation estimations, but requires assessing the full model solutions.

Model simulation

This section uses Newton's method for solving dynamic simultaneous equation systems (as implemented by Time Series Processor) to simulate the above system in a dynamic setting. The first subsection uses in-sample simulations to evaluate the models dynamic properties. The second subsection then presents the dynamic response of the model to debt shocks, and the final subsection uses the same techniques to evaluate historically the effects of the recent US debt expansion on international financial markets.

Model evaluation

The most important, and strongest, test of a structural model containing simultaneous equations is to examine its dynamic simulation properties. The model as a whole must be able to track historical data and must have reasonable dynamic properties. As already mentioned, many versions of the model, while providing very good single-equation statistics, were not able to produce overall simulation results that could be considered acceptable.

Summary simulation statistics for the final model are presented in Table 6.3. To provide an even better feel for the ability of the model to track actual data, Figures 6.1 to 6.6 show the actual against fitted values for the in-sample simulation. The expected real exchange rate (which is just a weighted average of the relative goods prices) has a reasonably low Theil statistic of 0.178. This was encouraging, given that the expected goods-market exchange rate provides an important anchor for the actual financial real exchange rate. The model was not able to pick up the exact quarterly fluctuations in this variable, as shown in Figure 6.1, although it does show very similar overall trends. For example, the measured expected real exchange rate fell by around 21 per cent in the first seven years of the floating-rate period, while the simulated value showed a fall of 18 per cent over the same period. In the period from 1980 to 1985 the expected real exchange rate rose by 14 per cent, while the simulated value rose by just over 6 per cent. A major disappointment was the inability of the model to pick turning points in the expected exchange rate. In

Table 6.3 Simulation statistics

| Statistics | Variables | | | | | |
	$E\bar{e}$	r	r^*	e	ca	ca^*
RMSE	0.044	0.796	1.230	0.081	6.266	4.832
Theil	0.178	0.072	0.146	0.158	0.578	0.157

Note: The statistics are calculated from a dynamic within-sample simulation, that is, 1973:2 to 1985:4.

Figure 6.1 The expected real exchange rate: actual against fitted values

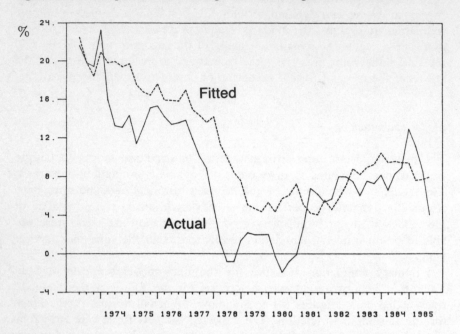

Figure 6.2 The non-US real interest rate: actual against fitted values

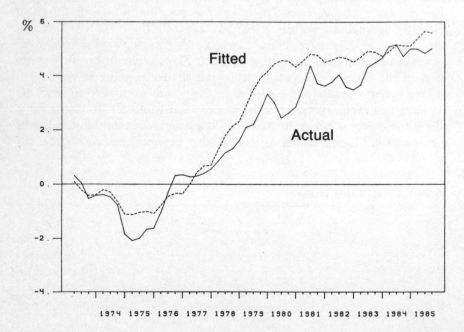

Figure 6.3 The US real interest rate: actual against fitted values

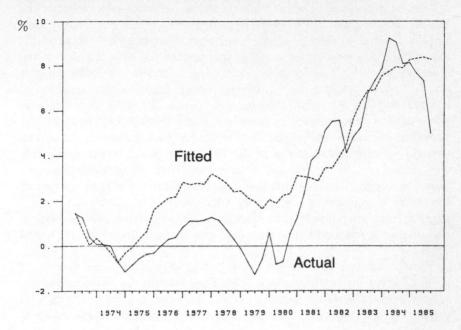

particular, it does not capture the sharp turnaround that occurred in 1985:1.

The two interest rates also have relatively good in-sample tracking ability. The non-US rate, in Figure 6.2, tracks quite well the fall in real interest rates in the early 1970s and the subsequent rise during the late 1970s and 1980s. It ends up well above its actual value by the end of the 1970s, but returns to the actual data by the end of the sample, indicating no permanent instability. Like the expected exchange rate, the non-US interest rate does not predict quarterly turning points. This is not surprising given the difficulty of modelling short-run financial market fluctuations. The ability of the model to pick up general trends is, however, quite good as is shown by the low Theil statistic for the non-US interest rate.

The US rate (Figure 6.3) exhibits similar patterns to the non-US one, overshooting the level of interest rates through much of the 1970s, but still capturing general trends. Important for the overall model simulations (especially for the exchange rate) is the fact that the model does reproduce much of the rise in US real interest rates in the period 1980–5. It should be remembered that the higher RMSE for the US interest rate is not just a reflection of poor model performance, but also reflects the higher and more volatile pattern of actual rates over the sample period. The Theil statistic for the US interest rate is reasonable at 0.146.

The current real exchange rate provides very good in-sample tracking, relative to what one expects from empirical exchange-rate models. The RMSE, at less than 10 per cent, is comparable to the very early results for the Federal Reserve's MCM,[26] although Hooper (1986) reports that the MCM (like most other models) was unable to track the rise in the dollar up to 1985. Most model-builders seem reluctant to publish statistics on the recent tracking ability of the major multi-country models, so comparisons for the whole floating-rate period are difficult.[27] Plots of actual against simulated values from our model (Figure 6.4) show that the simulated exchange rate peaked in 1985:1 after having appreciated by just over 40 per cent from the end of the 1970s; the actual real exchange rate also peaked in 1985:1 but had risen by just over 50 per cent from its previous trough. The fact that the model does explain a large portion of the dollar's appreciation, with only such meager specification, strongly suggests that government debt does have an important role to play in explaining the substantial real exchange-rate fluctuations of the 1970s and 1980s.

Finally, the two current account variables (Figures 6.5 and 6.6) show quite different in-sample tracking. The Theil statistic for the non-US bloc is very poor. This result seems to come from the large negative sign on the net foreign asset term discussed above, which generates large cycles in

Figure 6.4 The real exchange rate: actual against fitted values

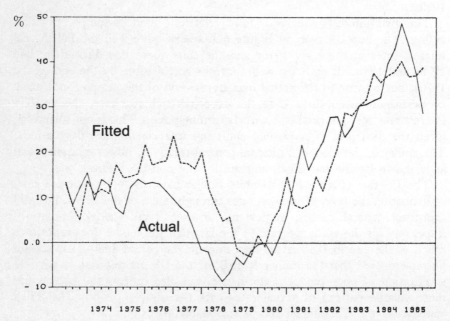

Figure 6.5 The non-US current account: actual against fitted values

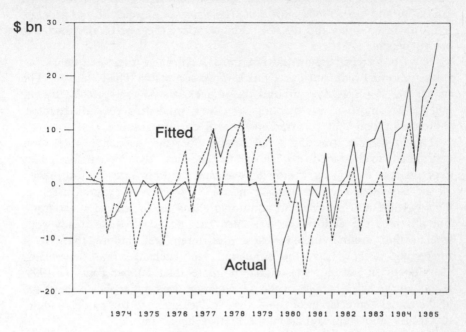

Figure 6.6 The US current account: actual against fitted values

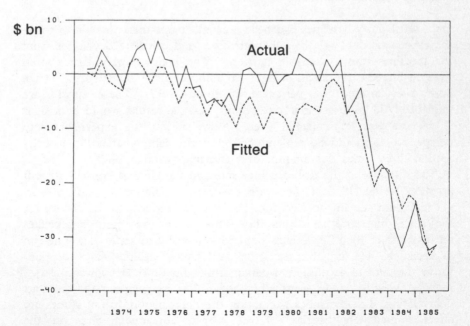

this variable. Major deviations occurred from the actual values around the late 1970s and early 1980s. However, the short-term cycles do not generate long-run instabilities and do not seem to affect the rest of the model to a great extent.

The US current account did not show such severe short-run deviations from the actual data and has a much more acceptable Theil statistic. The model was again weakest around the late 1970s and early 1980s. By the end of the sample it was tracking very well, predicting the full extent of the deterioration that occurred in the US current account.

The in-sample tracking, particularly for the exchange rate, was considered to be adequate to go on and use the model for policy experiments. To do this, the model was simulated out into the future with all the exogenous variables held at their 1985:4 values to create a baseline. This baseline also provided an additional check on the model's stability.[28] For all cases the endogenous variables had settled to their steady state level within around fifteen years, and often well before that. It is interesting to note that the simulated real exchange rate depreciated sharply out of sample, weakening by more than 50 per cent by 1990. Although the exact pattern of the depreciation does not replicate the speed of the actual depreciation of the dollar, it does point to the model's ability to capture important trends in the real exchange rate.

Rising government debt

Once satisfactory baselines had been created, it was then possible to shock the exogenous debt variables in both blocs and calculate deviations from the baselines over reasonable horizons. The policy experiments chosen were to increase the stock of debt in both countries by 10 per cent (in both cases around 3.5 per cent of trend GNP). These shocks are implausibly large to occur in one period, but the results would be similar if the rise was implemented over a year; to put the experiment into perspective it should be remembered that US debt outstanding rose by around three times this amount over the five years to 1985.

The response of the real exchange rate and the US and non-US current accounts to the US debt shock are presented in Figures 6.7 and 6.8. In general, both the impact and long-run results conform to the theory for the case of high asset substitutability. The exchange-rate jump appreciates on impact and then depreciates non-monotonically to settle at a long-run depreciation. The initial appreciation and higher wealth (via absorption) throw the current account into deficit; this runs down net foreign assets; reduces wealth; and eventually leads the exchange rate to start depreciating. The dynamics generating the depreciation do not come into effect immediately because of the lagged adjustment term in the

Figure 6.7 US debt shock: exchange-rate response

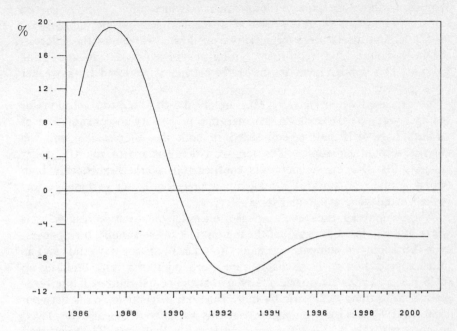

Figure 6.8 US debt shock: current account responses

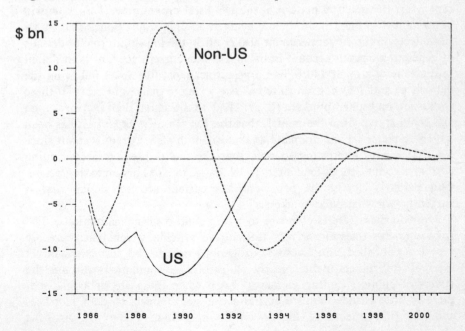

interest-rate equation. The exchange also starts depreciating because it has jumped up above the expected long-run rate (which appreciates by less on impact). The exchange rate settles at a long-run steady-state depreciation as net foreign assets are substantially run down, worsening the interest-income account, and requiring a long-run improvement in the trade balance. The improvement in the trade balance is achieved by a weaker exchange rate.

As discussed extensively by Masson (1986), the long-run solution for the exchange rate depends on the marginal propensity to consume out of wealth. This coefficient is embedded in both the interest rate and the current account equations. The long-run depreciation of the US dollar suggests that, for our model, this coefficient is neither excessively high (which would lead towards a long-run appreciation), nor excessively low (which could generate model instability).[29]

Without putting excessive emphasis on exact quantitative results, it is worth looking, in more detail, at the magnitudes of the simulated responses, even if it is only to compare the model to other multi-country studies. The initial appreciation of the exchange rate is around 10 per cent, building up to 19 per cent after six quarters. Given that the actual ratio of US government debt to trend GNP rose by more than ten percentage points between 1980 and 1985 it is easy to imagine that this rise in government debt played an important role in the dollar appreciation over that time. The suggested multiplier actually indicates that the build-up in debt may account for even more of the actual appreciation, although a formal evaluation requires replicating the exacting pattern of the US fiscal programme. This issue will be examined in more detail below using in-sample simulations. The short-run effects on the current account also confirm the important role of deficits in generating current account imbalances. The current account is in deficit to the tune of around $40 billion a year for almost five years following the debt shock and does not return to balance for more than eight years. If these results are multiplied by three (to get close to the actual debt increase) then one could argue (from the model) that the Reagan debt expansion has been largely to blame for the dramatic weakening of the US current account since 1980. It is also interesting to note that the model predicts a continuing current account deficit, long after the exchange rate has begun to depreciate. This parallels closely the persistent US current account deficit that is currently worrying policy-makers.

How do these results compare to other multi-country simulations? The answer to this question is very difficult to provide, given that there are very few published simulations of exogenous rises in the permanent target level of government debt. Nearly all published simulations discuss the effects of public spending increases. Even when these are debt-financed, there is little chance of distinguishing the stock effects of debt increases and the flow effects of higher public spending.[30] There is also the problem that policy experiments are always slightly different across models, and it is difficult to know whether 'add factors' have been extensively employed to produce sensible results.

Despite these problems, there is some agreement on the medium-run effects of a US fiscal expansion on the exchange rate, as was pointed out in Chapter 3. In most simulations of a US fiscal expansion, there is generally an appreciation of the exchange rate within the first two years, although by varying amounts. This result comes out very clearly from the comparative Brookings study reported above (Frankel 1986). The multipliers reported there ranged from a nominal appreciation of 4 per cent for the Taylor model to a depreciation of 2.1 per cent for the Wharton model (following a rise of one percentage point in the government-spending to GNP ratio.)[31] If one takes an average of these results of around 2 per cent and then multiplies by three (to come close to the size of the above policy experiment) then it is clear that our results show a somewhat larger, but still reasonable, exchange-rate response to a US fiscal shock.

Turning to the two models that are small enough to 'see through' and that were discussed in detail in Chapter 4, one sees a much closer agreement in results. The Knight and Masson (1985) model gives an impact (one year) appreciation of just over 5.5 per cent for a one percentage point of GNP rise in the budget deficit; multiplying by three produces a result very close to our six quarter (19 per cent) maximum appreciation. As in our model, the Knight and Masson simulations show a steady depreciation over the long run. The Knight and Masson results are also similar for the current account, except that their model produces the disturbing result that the current account goes further into deficit in the long run. MINIMOD produces the same general picture. The exchange rate appreciates by around 2 per cent on impact, then depreciates over the dynamic adjustment.[32]

The results for the fiscal shock in the non-US bloc provide a somewhat different picture. In Figure 6.9 the exchange-rate response is shown. The exchange rate appreciates on impact, but by much less than in the US debt-shock case. The initial appreciation peaks at just under 9 per cent after five quarters, and the exchange rate then begins to depreciate. It eventually moves to a long-run appreciation of around 3 per cent. This result is consistent with the theory for the case where domestic bonds are poor substitutes for foreign asset. Even though the domestic interest rate rises sharply after the fiscal expansion,[33] the exchange rate only appreciates slightly on impact. This is because the higher level of domestic bonds creates a risk premium, ensuring that the exchange rate need not be expected to depreciate by the full amount of the interest differential (as in the US case). In this way the domestic interest rate (and by implication absorption) is forced to bear the burden of higher debt to a much greater degree.

Figure 6.9 Non-US debt shock: exchange-rate response

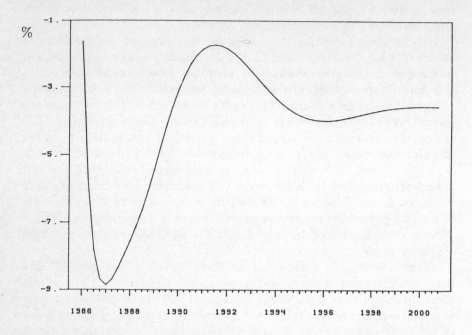

Figure 6.10 Non-US debt shock: current account responses

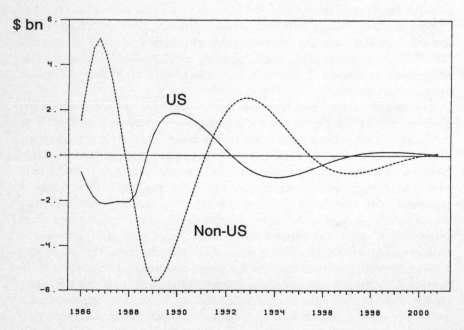

The dynamic adjustment is largely governed by the current account response, shown in Figure 6.10. The non-US current account actually goes into surplus on impact after the rise in non-US debt. This is probably due to the strong 'J-curve' effects in the non-US current account and to the very strong rise in the non-US interest rate, reducing domestic absorption. There is little tendency for net foreign assets to fall in the long run in the non-US bloc, a sharply different result to the US debt-expansion case. This allows the real exchange rate to appreciate in the long run, as domestic absorption is lowered by a long-run increase in the real interest rate. (The trade balance would tend to go into surplus if there were not a long-run appreciation.)

In contrast to the previous US case, long-run crowding-out in the non-US block is not of net foreign assets but of domestic capital. This result stems largely from the different role that US versus non-US assets play in the international financial system. Other important factors generating asymmetries are the differing current account responses to exchange-rate changes and differing wealth effects in goods markets across countries. These asymmetries have major implications for fiscal policy co-ordination, which will be discussed in more detail in Chapter 7.[34]

Comparing the model's exchange rate results for the non-US fiscal shock with those discussed in Frankel (1986) is not easy. There is wide disagreement reported for the non-US fiscal shock, ranging from an appreciation of the non-US currencies of over 3 per cent to depreciations of up to 2.5 per cent. In contrast, the MINIMOD and Knight and Masson models, having symmetric asset-demand equations, show similar exchange-rate and current account responses no matter where the deficit originates, that is, an impact appreciation and a long-run depreciation. Our results fit somewhere near the average of many of the other models.

Evaluating US fiscal policy

The above debt shocks point to the financing aspects of fiscal policy as being of major importance to international capital market stability. This subsection takes such a hypothesis one step further by trying to evaluate — quantitatively — the recent historical role of US fiscal policy in generating financial market instability. To do this, the two-country model is simulated under the assumption that the United States did not embark on a major supply-side fiscal policy package in the early 1980s. Specifically, it is assumed that the US debt-to-GNP ratio remained at its end of 1979 level throughout the sample period, while other exogenous variables are left at their actual levels.[35] The actual experiment is somewhat unrealistic. If US fiscal policy were changed so drastically, it is likely that other policy variables, particularly non-US variables, would also be altered. However, the experiment is not designed to reproduce likely real-world behaviour. It should rather be seen as generating a baseline against which one can compare actual outcomes.

The most interesting results are presented in Figures 6.11 to 6.13. Looking first at the real exchange rate, the model suggests that, if there had been no expansion of the US deficits and debt in the 1980s, the US dollar would not have swung wildly as has been the case. The simulated exchange rate appreciates only by around 9 per cent from the end of 1979 level and this occurs by early 1981 (a period of tight monetary policy in the United States). The quantitative results are clearly not an extremely powerful test of the Ricardian Equivalence Theorem, but are certainly evidence against the argument that tax-financed deficits have no real effects. The main conclusion to be drawn from the model is that the recent fiscal expansion in the United States has been at least partially responsible for the growing instabilities in international financial markets (documented in Chapter 1).

The interest-rate results also support this interpretation. The simulated US interest rate is shown in Figure 6.12. Unlike the actual interest rate, which rose rapidly to record level over the 1980s, the simulated rate rises only slowly. Moreover, it stabilizes at around 3 per cent, a level that is

Figure 6.11 Constant US debt: exchange-rate response

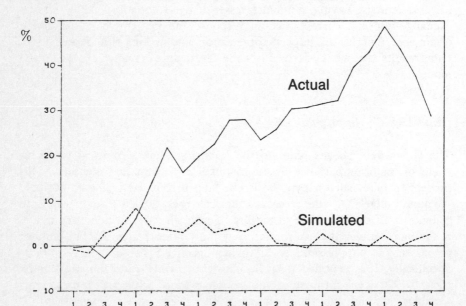

Figure 6.12 Constant US debt: US interest-rate response

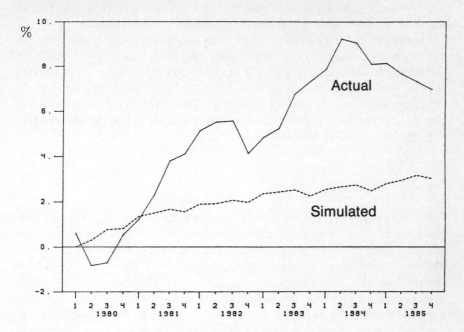

Figure 6.13 Constant US debt: US current account response

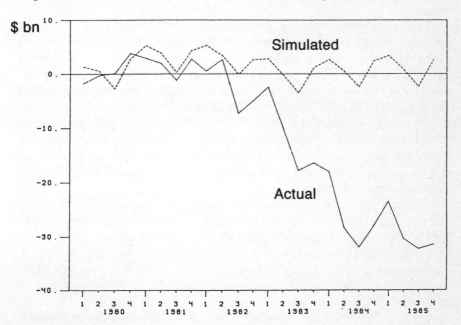

close to the average since the 1960s. The evidence is again strongly against the debt-neutrality hypothesis that predicts no real effects of changes in the level of debt for a given amount of government spending.

Finally, Figure 6.13 presents the current account results. Here, too, the model suggests that the rise in US debt has been largely responsible for the huge deterioration in the US current account. Over the simulated sample, the current account remains basically balanced, with even a slight tendency towards a surplus in the early 1980s. Although not shown, the current account for the non-US countries is also stabilized by the elimination of the US fiscal imbalance.

Possible extensions

The two-country model estimated and simulated in this chapter has provided substantial insights into the issues of real exchange-rate determination and the role of international fiscal policy in generating cross-country disturbances in financial markets. These issues could not be analysed in the world-economy framework of Chapter 5. The added complication of splitting the industrial countries into two blocs has been very rewarding. The world is, of course, made up of many countries and the most obvious extension to the model would be to attempt to break the non-US sector into its six component countries. Explicitly adding the OPEC and developing countries would also allow many more issues to be examined.

Another alternative way of extending the analysis would be to explore, in more detail, particular sectors of the model. Development of the monetary sector, with the inclusion of an endogenous inflation rate, would certainly provide more realism and enable the links between monetary and fiscal policy to be modelled explicitly. A final area that requires further work is that of expectations formation. A useful way of proceeding would be to try and estimate the model using different assumptions regarding expectations and see if this affected the general conclusions. All of these extensions are important, but, one lesson from this study is that it may not be sensible (or feasible) to include all aspects of the real world in every empirical test undertaken.

To close this chapter, it should be stressed that the quantitative results are not meant to reflect the exact response of financial markets to debt shocks, but to give a qualitative feel for likely effects of permanent policy changes. Many of the multipliers, particularly for the long-run, are not in the reasonable range and the results are probably best interpreted as medium-term. The lack of capital formation makes any interpretation of the long-run effects of debt rather difficult.[36] Finally, the general results do seem to be robust to a number of minor model-specification changes, although the long-run solutions to alternative specifications are not always stable.

Notes

1. The Venice Summit was most explicit on this, but co-ordinated fiscal decisions (or at least announcements) have become more frequent since the US budget moved sharply into deficit in the early 1980s.
2. See Aliber (1973) for the early theoretical work on the determinants of risk. Dooley and Isard (1980) provide evidence on the role of political risk in generating deviations from interest parity.
3. One simplifying assumption used in this specification is the lack of an explicit interest-income term in the absorption function. This is primarily because of data limitations.
4. In Dornbusch, this approach was used only to explain nominal exchange-rate expectations.
5. In the rest of the chapter all relative prices and the exchange rate are written in logs.
6. See Kole (1986) for a complete derivation. This form of the portfolio balance equation is also applied by Branson (1986).
7. Further discussion of these tests was provided in Chapter 4.
8. This seems to be a common problem in many large macro-models which may be estimated over periods when consumption may have been a very large share of — or even exceeded — disposable income. The problem is probably aggravated in our case because absorption is not split into its components.
9. See the work of Isard (1977) and Genberg (1978). The justification for slow adjustment may be derived from the usual overlapping wage-contracts explanation or by the role of imperfect competition, which Dornbusch (1987) has emphasized in explaining deviations from the law of one price.
10. There would need to be two terms-of-trade equations in the empirical model in any case because the data set employed does not cover the entire world. The product of the US terms of trade and the non-US bloc terms of trade is not equal to unity. For the same reason, there are two current account and net foreign asset equations in the empirical model. There is therefore an implicit exogenous third bloc that is not modelled, but which impacts on the US and non-US blocs.
11. In equations (6.21) to (6.26), for each domestic equation (including the current account and the terms of trade) there is a foreign country equation, although parameters are not constrained to be equal across countries. The identities in equations (6.1) to (6.12) are also used in the estimated and simulation procedures.
12. In particular, the government spending variables in the empirical model are no longer spending on the individual goods (because of data limitations), but are aggregate spending measures.
13. To calculate the expected real exchange rate empirically, it is necessary to weight together the four relative goods prices by their consumption shares. These shares have been assumed to be equal across countries. Sensitivity analysis confirmed that the results were robust to most reasonable values for the consumption shares.
14. The problems with the interest rate may also have resulted because they

should enter the current account in a non-linear way (depending on the size and sign of net foreign assets).

15. This issue is explored more fully by Stockman (1983) and Mussa (1986).

16. The exchange rate is always reported so that a rise represents an appreciation of the US dollar. To be consistent with the theory, the United States is therefore modelled as the foreign country.

17. Appendix A outlines, in more detail, the sources of the net foreign asset bench-mark positions (when they were available).

18. See Ott (1987), where it is argued that alternative weighting schemes make little difference to the results obtained from exchange-rate models.

19. The Durbin–Watson statistics may be biased upwards for those equations that contain lagged endogenous variables.

20. The oil price also impacts on the exchange rate indirectly via interest rate and wealth effects.

21. The annual estimations generally showed a greater number of significant coefficients.

22. The use of standard correction techniques, when serial correlation results from misspecification, may introduce even more inefficiencies into the coefficient estimation than the serial correlation itself. See Thursby (1987) for a recent discussion of these problems.

23. The one consistent coefficient was on the interest differential. It was always the expected sign and generally highly significant.

24. This is, of course, only true for the period under estimation. The true portfolio balance relationship is a non-linear one; it is unlikely that the private sectors would continue to absorb US dollar assets into their portfolios indefinitely.

25. The multicollinearity point is supported by the fact that the interest differential coefficient rises sharply (as does its significance) when the bond stocks are removed from the equation.

26. See Stevens *et al.* (1984) where RMSEs of around 10 per cent are reported for the period to 1975.

27. The length of the sample period is very important as dynamic simulations generally cumulate errors over time.

28. The TSP programme, used for estimation and simulation, does not calculate eigenvalues. The long-run simulation of the model provided an alternative strong test for stability. See Wallis and Whitley (1986), where alternative methodologies for evaluating the long-run properties of econometric models are discussed.

29. Masson (1986) traced instabilities in the MINIMOD to a low marginal propensity to consume out of wealth. In a number of other simulations, the MINIMOD builders reset this coefficient to produce more sensible long-run model behaviour.

30. Such simulation experiments often run into problems of long-run instabilities that arise because a permanent (debt-financed) rise in public spending generally implies explosive debt growth unless tax rates are also changed. For this reason, results are normally only reported for the short to medium term. See Masson (1986), where the inclusion of tax adjustment rule is shown to be crucial for the stability of a model that includes rational expectations. Our model does not face this problem because the level of debt is an exogenously targeted variable (which is also true in the long run for any stable model).

31. The movements in relative consumer prices were generally very small and often reinforced the effects of the nominal rate on the real exchange rate.

32. The size of the MINIMOD multipliers seems to be very sensitive to the exact specification of the model. See again the sensitivity analysis in Masson (1985).
33. It rises even more than in the US case.
34. Oudiz and Sachs (1984) emphasize this asymmetry in their multi-country model, although their coefficients are not estimated.
35. The constant debt-to-trend-GNP ratio does not imply a balanced budget, but represents a small nominal deficit over the simulation period.
36. The possible role of capital formation is discussed in Appendix B.

Chapter 7

Policy Conclusions

Introduction

The aim of this chapter is not to summarize all the results and conclusions of the previous chapters. Rather, it will apply the empirical models and their results to some concrete policy issues, issues that stand out as being both relevant and unresolved, not only amongst academics, but also amongst policy-makers. They include: the role of central banks in deciding on and trying to influence 'equilibrium' real exchange rates; and the role of co-ordinated fiscal policy in addressing international economic imbalances. The two issues are closely related and are both tied up with the question of what is the appropriate international financial system.

The second aim of the chapter is to attempt to bring together the very different empirical approaches taken so far. As shown theoretically by Aoki (1983) and Turnovsky (1986), there are advantages to thinking of a multi-country world as being composed of two separate dynamic systems. The first, the aggregate world system, is just the sum of the individual components. The second is the system of differences between the individual countries, which determines dynamics in bilateral variables such as exchange rates and current accounts. This work has so far employed the Aoki type of approach in an empirical setting.[1] The advantages of splitting the world model into averages and differences should not, however, lead to the conclusion that they are totally separate systems; both are different expressions of the same system.

We start by addressing the question of real exchange-rate determination. The two-country model is used to judge numerically the issue of appropriate exchange-rate regimes. Specifically, a fixed exchange rate or 'target zone' is imposed on the model and the resulting paths of the major endogenous variables are evaluated. We then turn to the policy coordination debate, stressing the importance of medium-term effects of short-run policy co-ordination, especially the links between bilateral policy imbalances and 'world' policy responses. We conclude by drawing some more general conclusions from the empirical work and outline areas where further research should be rewarding.

Exchange-rate targeting

The role of central banks in setting or targeting the appropriate level of the real exchange rate has always been controversial in a system of primarily floating nominal exchange rates. It was originially argued that the floating-rate system would largely aid in the adjustment of the economy towards equilibrium. In practice, there is now widespread belief that a floating-rate system may induce or condone the occurrence of disequilibrium in the economy.

The disappointment with the operation of the current floating-rate system hinges on the interpretation of the wild swings in exchange rates since the early 1970s as being largely a disequilibrium phenomenon. In particular, deviations from a very general definition of purchasing power parity are seen to be the result of unstable asset markets which do not relate the value of the exchange rate to fundamentals. The alternative view argues that financial market volatility is an equilibrium phenomenon and would point to other exogenous factors outside asset markets, as being the cause of the instability. The empirical results from Chapter 6 point to a large portion of the medium-term instability in real exchange rates (that is, deviations from purchasing power parity) being the result of: equilibrium changes in relative goods prices both across and within countries; and unstable public policy behaviour. Indeed, a relatively simple structural model, based only on a few fundamentals, tracked recent financial market instability reasonably well.

This is not to say there is no role for central bank intervention to try and smooth turbulent asset markets. The model was not able to reproduce all of the dollar's quarterly fluctuations,[2] nor all of the massive appreciation until 1985:1. This indicates that speculative forces, not captured in the model, may have been important in driving up the dollar. It is also true, however, that the missing speculative forces may have been pushing the dollar towards it true equilibrium. No model can capture accurately the role of forward-looking expectations and these may play an important part in moving asset markets towards their equilibrium values.

Whether or not central banks should or should not play some role in the short-run exchange-market smoothing operations is a very different question to the issue of targeting the appropriate real exchange rate. Much recent policy debate has revolved around the need to return to a system of fixed exchange rates, or at least to a system of target zones (see Williamson 1985; McKinnon 1984). Related to these ideas has been the growing belief, reflected in many policy announcements, that the US dollar can be targeted at a level to eliminate recent current account imbalances. The assumption appears to be that it is possible to 'talk the dollar' to any level required to remove the US current account deficit. Such a policy is often presented as an alternative to solving the budgetary impasse in the United States.

To examine these exchange-rate targeting issues more formally, the two-country model was simulated from 1980, under the assumption that the non-US bloc attempted to target the exchange rate over the remainder of the sample period. As the model was not designed to operate under a fixed-rate system, it has to be tricked into thinking that the exchange rate was being targeted.[3] This was done in two ways. In both it was assumed that the real exchange could be held constant for the period 1980:1 to 1985:4, thus removing the huge real appreciation that occurred over this time. In one version the exchange rate was held constant by endogenizing foreign exchange reserves in the non-US bloc. The required intervention was assumed to be fully sterilized. The second approach endogenized non-US public debt policy. This allowed non-US debt to expand, raising non-US interest rates just enough to prevent any incipient outflow of capital into US assets.

The required changes in these two policy variables to keep the exchange rate fixed are shown in Figures 7.1 and 7.2. Figure 7.1 shows plots of the actual level of non-US reserves against the simulated levels. It is immediately obvious that a policy of pure intervention by the non-US bloc could not have been feasible over the 1980–5 period. The required intervention would have wiped out all foreign exchange reserves by 1981 and implied foreign borrowing by the central banks to the tune of $500 billion by 1985. It is interesting to note that the required intervention amounts to the non-US central banks basically buying up all of the US government debt expansion over the period, again confirming the importance of the US debt expansion for the dollar's appreciation. Given that pure intervention does not appear to have been a feasible way to stabilize the exchange rate over the period under examination, one can conclude that any successful exchange-rate targeting arrangements will need to involve all major countries and would almost certainly require some form of macroeconomic policy responses to ensure targets were to be attainable. This is the basis of the second form of targeting policy.

The main point obtained from endogenizing non-US fiscal policy is that it also requires a similar large change in relative asset stocks to stabilize the dollar. In Figure 7.2 the needed rise in non-US debt is shown. By the end of the sample the non-US debt-to-GNP ratio is up by fourteen percentage points, even more than the rise in the US debt stock over the same horizon. Such a policy strategy is clearly a possible one, but it is certainly not one most governments would choose. The reason for this (shown in Figure 7.3), is that the required fiscal expansion would have raised non-US interest rates to what were clearly unacceptable levels (around 13 per cent).

What is perhaps even more interesting for current policy debates is the response of the US current account to the fixed exchange-rate regime. Despite the fact that the exchange rate is held constant over the 1980–5

Figure 7.1 Fixed exchange rate: non-US foreign exchange reserves

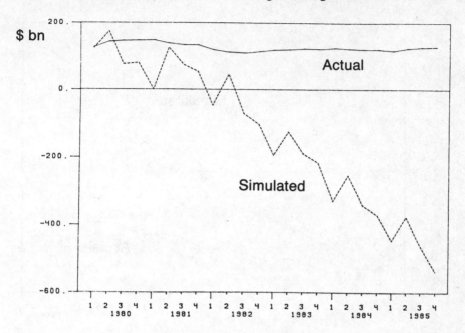

Figure 7.2 Fixed exchange rates: the non-US debt response

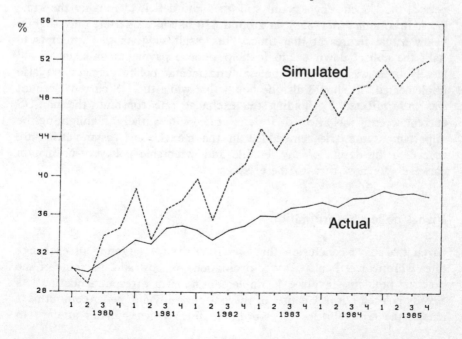

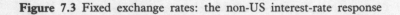

Figure 7.3 Fixed exchange rates: the non-US interest-rate response

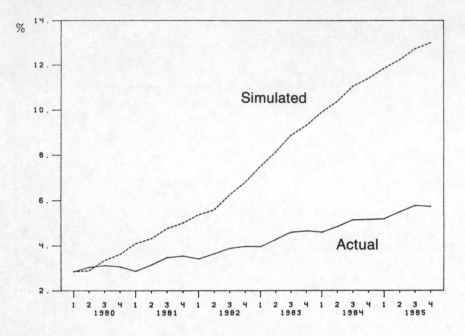

period, the US current account still goes into deficit to roughly the same level. It bottoms, in 1985:3, at around $30 billion a quarter, only slightly below actual figures at that time. This result suggests that attempts to 'talk the dollar' down or up to help remove payments imbalances will largely be a waste of time unless fundamental policy changes are also implemented.[4] It should also be noted that while the US current account was little affected by holding the exchange rate constant, the non-US current account was affected. It deteriorated substantially, highlighting the important asymmetries embedded in the model. Such asymmetries are crucial to the design of any feasible and acceptable policy co-ordination package. We now turn to these issues.

Fiscal policy co-ordination

Given the above conclusion that any international targeting of exchange rates will involve fiscal policy co-ordination, we now address some of the practical problems involved in implementing such a recommendation. As already pointed out in Chapter 6, there is currently a growing commitment among the G7 countries to co-ordinate fiscal policies in an attempt to alleviate the current account imbalances that are apparently threatening the stability of the world's financial system. To date, the policy commitments agreed upon have centred primarily upon the United States' cutting its budget deficit, with the major non-US countries providing for an increase in the budget deficits to offset the negative impact on world aggregate demand from the cuts to the US deficit.

Such a strategy clearly implies that there are symmetric and offsetting effects of the two fiscal measures on the world-economy average target variables (income and real interest rates). It also assumes that such co-ordinated measures can eliminate bilateral imbalances, particularly current account imbalances. It was argued in Chapter 6 that attempts to push West Germany and Japan to expand their already high levels of govern-ment debt would have little impact on current account imbalances and only tend to push up non-US real interest rates. In this section the effects of coordinated fiscal policy are examined formally, by simulating a co-ordinated fiscal policy package. In doing so, attention is given both to asymmetries and to effects such a package might have on the world average endogenous variables.

The policy package is based on the type of aggreement announced after the Venice Summit meeting — the US should lower it budget deficit, while the non-US countries (particularly Japan and West Germany) should undertake expansionary fiscal policy. The exact simulation is of a one percentage point of GNP rise in debt in the non-US bloc and a one percentage point of GNP reduction of debt in the United States. The size of the policy shocks was chosen to reflect the most optimistic view possi-ble of the Venice Summit commitments.[5]

Figure 7.4 indicates that the combined policy action would have the desired effect on the US current account deficit. However, the initial effects are small and, even after five years, the maximum improvement in the current account is only $5 billion a quarter. The size of the required policy adjustment package to eliminate the US payments imbalance would need to be much larger and more sustained than the one undertaken. The major reason for the small response of the US current account is that the effects of the non-US debt expansion are not symmetric to the effects of the US debt expansion, as was stressed in Chapter 6. The effects of the non-US debt expansion work mainly on domestic non-US financial markets; pushing up non-US interest rates and (implicitly) depressing domestic demand. This rise in interest rates does not impact on the exchange rate because of the risk premium added to the holding of non-US bonds. The nature of the asymmetries is shown by the fact that the non-US current account actually goes into surplus after the policy-co-ordination shock.

Both the US and non-US interest-rate responses are shown in Figure 7.5. The US interest rate falls on impact, but then slowly rises to a

Figure 7.4 Co-ordinated fiscal policy: the current account responses

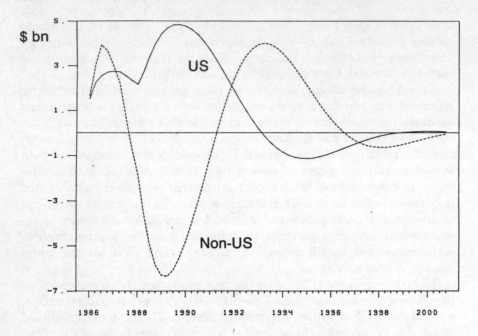

Figure 7.5 Coordinated fiscal policy: the interest rate response

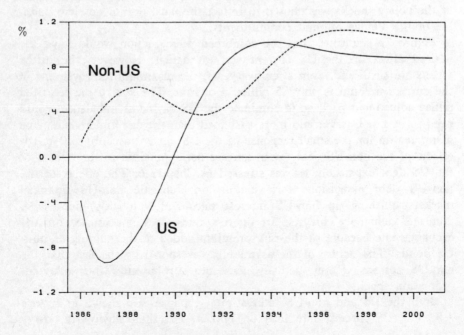

level around one percentage point above the baseline. In contrast, the non-US rate rises over the whole simulation, eventually by more than the US rate. The medium-term implication from the policy package is therefore a rise in real interest rates in the world as a whole, but especially in the non-US bloc. Here then, is a major negative impact on the world as a whole from a policy package that should have no impact on world averages, under the assumptions of symmetric economies. If these results are correct, one can understand the reluctance of the West German and Japanese policy-makers to embark on expansionary fiscal policies as a means of combating world payments imbalances. Indeed, the major policy conclusion from this chapter is that addressing the US current account problem should be done at the source, that is, by correcting the US fiscal policy impasse. Drawing the other major countries into the policy debate will mainly divert attention from the primary issue. It may, following the above simulations, even aggravate the problem in the short run.

Finally, the co-ordinated fiscal policy experiment has also implications for the real exchange rate and the issue of exchange-rate targeting. In the long run the US dollar appreciates, as most commentators would expect, from such a package. In the short run, however, the dollar depreciates by nearly 10 per cent, something that would be at odds with current attempts to prevent large short-run fluctuations in real exchange rates, the point being that current attempts to hold the dollar within a narrow predetermined range may be inconsistent with the goal of reducing the US current account deficit via fiscal policy management. The US dollar may need to depreciate even further in the short-run, as a means of reaching a sustainable current account and a stronger exchange rate in the long run. In other words, fiscal policy co-ordination is a prerequisite for exchange-rate targeting, but exchange-rate targeting is not a prerequisite for the stabilization of international financial markets via a co-ordinated fiscal policy.

Conclusions

The fundamental conclusion of this book, following the evidence in the last three chapters, must be that alternative financing of public sector spending has important implications for international financial markets. Evidence supporting the Ricardian Equivalence Theorem was not found, either in world or domestic asset markets. Why are these results so consistent and so strong, while many other studies find support for the debt neutrality proposition? Some possible reasons for this (derived in the first two theoretical chapters) are:

1. The importance that integrated capital markets play in the empirical tests of debt neutrality. In all of our empirical work above, the possibility of international capital mobility has been explicitly allowed for, something that is generally not done in the literature.
2. The need to include the stock effects of deficits, as well as the flow impact stressed in traditional macroeconomics.
3. The use of real rather than nominal debt (or deficits) which is not very common in other studies.
4. The specification of structural models that allow for strong tests of debt neutrality, rather than the use of *ad hoc* reduced-form equations containing all possible fiscal variables.
5. Finally, the study has used recent data incorporating a major debt expansion not associated with war, recession or government spending increases.

This book has also uncovered, or in some case supported, many other interesting issues along the way. In our 'world' model, the Fisher hypothesis was shown to receive much more support once inflationary expectations are aggregated across countries. The same model also indicated the importance of the oil shocks for explaining the observed negative real interest rates that occurred during the 1970s, something that has been suggested before but (to my knowledge) never tested.

The two-country model provided many insights into the determination of the real exchange rates and their dynamic behaviour over time. The model was able to track the historical path of the US dollar and real interest rates quite well, supporting the idea that medium-term financial market fluctuations are largely an equilibrium phenomenon. Shifts in relative goods prices were responsible for a large portion of the US dollar appreciation until 1985. The model also pointed to substantial overshooting in foreign exchange markets, but this aspect need not indicate inefficiencies in financial markets. Rather, such behaviour was exactly as predicted by the theoretical models discussed in Chapter 4.

The final policy conclusions to be drawn are straightforward. First, medium- or long-term targeting of exchange rates will be both difficult and perhaps even destabilizing without the explicit allowance for shifts in relative goods prices. Moreover, other aspects of public policy, particularly changes in debt finance, have played a major role in determining real exchange rates. The implication is that fiscal policy co-ordination and real exchange-rate targeting need to be part of the same policy-making process. Relying only on central bank intervention and 'jawboning' to maintain target zones is unlikely to be feasible in the medium term. Unfortunately, at the time of writing there is no indication that any of the major powers are willing (or able) to actively use fiscal policy to keep exchange rates stable. The outlook of the return to a more fixed system of exchange rates is therefore not very bright.[6]

Finally, even if a more active role for fiscal policy in international economic management can be achieved, it will need to be based on a much more complicated model than the simple symmetric type of analysis used to date. International financial markets do not appear to treat government securities from differing countries in the same way. As a result, budget deficits in different countries have assymetric impact on exchange rates, interest rates and current accounts.

Notes

1. The theoretical technique would not be exactly applicable to our model, which explicitly tries to capture asymmetries, something that is not possible theoretically.
2. Let alone the often extreme weekly and daily movements in exchange rates.
3. Over the long-run model, being specified in real terms, is not suited to a fixed exchange-rate interpretation, unless governments were to target relative goods prices as well.
4. The targeting experiment was also carried out *ex ante*, to evaluate the model's ability to track recent (largely successful) attempts to target the dollar. To do this, a forecasting version of the model was constructed with data being estimated up to the end of 1986 where they were otherwise not available. This version of the model showed almost the same tracking ability and dynamic simulation behaviour as the primary model. It was simulated from 1987 to 1990 holding the exchange rate (and the exogenous variables) constant. Non-US foreign exchange intervention was endogenized. The results pointed to a build-up of non-US foreign exchange of over $100 billion in the first three quarters of 1987, an amount that is comparable to recent estimates. The US current account remained in deficit, peaking at $40 billion a quarter in 1987:3, and it still showed a $25 billion deficit in 1990. Without the rise in intervention, model simulations suggest that the dollar would have fallen by a further 10 per cent in 1987.
5. No precise numbers on fiscal policy were produced at the Summit, and it seems likely that the United States, in particular, will not provide any large reductions in its deficit until after the 1988 presidential elections.
6. This does not rule out the possible usefulness of intervention policy to smooth out the basically random short-run fluctuations in nominal exchange rates.

Appendix A

Data sources

Variable	Country	Source	Comments
O	OPEC	IFS	Price of Saudi Arabian Light in US dollars
OP	OPEC	IFS	Current account of OPEC in US dollars
RES	US	IFS	Foreign exchange reserves (Line 1d.d)
$\underline{M}$	US	IFS	Narrow money (Line 34)
G	US	IFS	Government consumption of goods and services (Line 99f.c)
R	US	IFS	Long-term government bond yield (Line 61)
C_P	US	IFS	Consumer prices (Line 64)
P_h	US	IFS	Hourly wage rates (Line 65ey)
P_x	US	IFS	Export unit values (Line 74)
P_i	US	IFS	Import unit values (Line 75)
ca	US	IFS	Current account (Line 77azd)
nfa	US	IFS	Cumulated current account with bench-mark taken from Knight and Masson (1985), \$149.5 bn in 1982:4
b	US	IFS	Central government debt (Line 88) less central bank holdings of debt (Line 88aa) and non-US foreign exchange reserves (*res*)
GNP	US	IFS	Nominal gross national product (Line 99b)
s	US	IFS	Nominal capital stock, cumulated IFS private investment (Line 93e) from zero bench-mark in 1975. Depreciation was also set to zero.
e_N	Germany	IFS	Nominal exchange rate against US dollar (Line rf)
res	Germany	IFS	Foreign exchange reserves (Line 1d.d)
M	Germany	IFS	Narrow money (Line 34)
$\bar{g}$	Germany	IFS	Government consumption of goods and services (Line 99f)
r	Germany	IFS	Long-term government bond yield (Line 60b)
C_P	Germany	IFS	Consumer prices (Line 64)
P_h	Germany	IFS	Hourly wage rates (Line 65ey)
P_x	Germany	IFS	Export unit values (Line 76)
P_i	Germany	IFS	Import unit values (Line 75)
ca	Germany	IFS	Current account (Line 77azd)
nfa	Germany	IFS	Cumulated current account with benchmark taken from Knight and Masson (1985) as \$27.7 bn in 1982:4
b	Germany	IFS	Central government debt (Line 88 except latest observation which comes from BB), less central bank claims on govt. (Line 12a)
GNP	Germany	IFS	Nominal gross national product (Line 99b)
s	Germany	IFS	Nominal capital stock, cumulated IFS private investment (Line 93e) from zero bench-mark in 1975. Depreciation was also set to zero.
e_N	Japan	IFS	Nominal exchange rate against US dollar (Line rf)

Variable	Country	Source	Comments
res	Japan	IFS	Foreign exchange reserves (Line 1d.d)
m	Japan	IFS	Narrow money (Line 34)
$\bar{g}$	Japan	IFS	Government consumption of goods and services (Line 99f, except before 1965 and held as constant share of GNP)
r	Japan	IFS	Long-term government bond yield (Line 60b), data were not available between 1960 and 1965, and the changes in lending rate (Line 60p) were spliced onto the annual series
C_P	Japan	IFS	Consumer prices (Line 64)
P_h	Japan	IFS	Hourly wage rates (Line 65ey)
P_x	Japan	IFS	Export unit values (Line 74)
P_i	Japan	IFS	Import unit values (Line 75)
ca	Japan	IFS	Current account (Line 77azd)
nfa	Japan	IFS	Cumulated current account with bench-mark taken from Knight and Masson (1985) as \$24.7 bn in 1982:4
b	Japan	IFS	Central government debt (Line 88b, except for years after 1979 which were spliced using OECD figures. Quarterly data were obtained by linear interpolation) less central bank claims on govt. (Line 12a)
s	Japan	IFS	Nominal capital stock, cumulated IFS private investment (Line 93e) from zero bench-mark in 1975. Depreciation was also set to zero.
GNP	Japan	IFS	Nominal gross national product (Line 99b)
e_N	France	IFS	Nominal exchange rate against US dollar (Line rf)
res	France	IFS	Foreign exchange reserves (Line 1d.d)
m	France	IFS	Narrow money (Line 34)
$\bar{g}$	France	IFS	Government consumption of goods and services (Line 99f)
r	France	IFS	Long-term government bond yield (Line 61)
C_P	France	IFS	Consumer prices (Line 64)
P_h	France	IFS	Labour costs (Line 65)
P_x	France	IFS	Export unit values (Line 74)
P_i	France	IFS	Import unit values (Line 75)
ca	France	IFS	Current account (Line 77azd)
nfa	France	IFS	Cumulated current account with bench-mark set to zero in 1968:1
b	France	IFS	Central government debt (Lines 88b and 89b) less central bank claims on govt. (Line 12a)
s	France	IFS	Nominal capital stock, cumulated IFS private investment (Line 93e) from zero bench-mark in 1975). Depreciation was also set to zero.
GNP	France	IFS	Nominal gross national product (Line 99b)
e_N	UK	IFS	Nominal exchange rate against US dollar (Line rh)
res	UK	IFS	Foreign exchange reserves (Line 1d.d)
m	UK	IFS	Narrow money (Line 34)
$\bar{g}$	UK	IFS	Government consumption of goods and services (Line 99f)
r	UK	IFS	Long-term government bond yield (Line 61)
C_P	UK	IFS	Consumer prices (Line 64)
P_h	UK	IFS	Average earnings (Line 65)
P_x	UK	IFS	Export unit values (Line 74)
P_i	UK	IFS	Import unit values (Line 75)
ca	UK	IFS	Current account (Line 77azd)
nfa	UK	IFS	Cumulated current account with bench-mark set to zero in 68:1
b	UK	IFS	Central government debt (cumulated central govt. deficit (Line 80) benchmark set at £25 bn in 1968:1 from CSO) less central bank claims on govt. (Line 12a)
s	UK	IFS	Nominal capital stock, cumulated IFS private investment (Line 93e) from zero benchmark in 1975). Depreciation was also set to zero.

Variable	Country	Source	Comments
GNP	UK	IFS	Nominal gross national product (Line 99b)
e_N	Italy	IFS	Nominal exchange rate against US dollar (Line rf)
res	Italy	IFS	Foreign exchange reserves (Line 1d.d)
m	Italy	IFS	Narrow money (Line 34)
$\bar{g}$	Italy	IFS	Government consumption of goods and services (Line 99f)
r	Italy	IFS	Long-term government bond yield (Line 61)
C_P	Italy	IFS	Consumer prices (Line 64)
P_h	Italy	IFS	Hourly wage rates (Line 65ey)
P_x	Italy	IFS	Export unit values (Line 74)
P_i	Italy	IFS	Import unit values (Line 75)
ca	Italy	IFS	Current account (Line 77azd)
nfa	Italy	IFS	Cumulated current account with bench-mark set to zero in 1968:1
b	Italy	IFS	Central government debt (Line 88) less central bank claims on govt. (Line 12a)
s	Italy	IFS	Nominal capital stock, cumulated IFS private investment (Line 93e) from zero bench-mark in 1975. Depreciation was also set to zero.
GNP	Italy	IFS	Nominal gross national product (Line 99b) 1985 estimated
e_N	Canada	IFS	Nominal exchange rate against US dollar (Line rf)
res	Canada	IFS	Foreign exchange reserves (Line 1d.d)
m	Canada	IFS	Narrow money (Line 34)
$\bar{g}$	Canada	IFS	Government consumption of goods and services (Line 99f)
r	Canada	IFS	Long-term government bond yield (Line 61)
C_P	Canada	IFS	Consumer prices (Line 64)
P_h	Canada	IFS	Hourly wage rates (Line 65ey)
P_x	Canada	IFS	Export unit values (Line 74)
P_i	Canada	IFS	Import unit values (Line 75)
ca	Canada	IFS	Current account (Line 77azd)
nfa	Canada	IFS	Cumulated current account with bench-mark set to zero in 1968:1
b	Canada	IFS	Central government debt (Line 88) less central bank holdings of debt (Line 88aa)
s	Canada	IFS	Nominal capital stock, cumulated IFS private investment (Line 93e) from zero bench-mark in 1975. Depreciation was also set to zero.
GNP	Canada	IFS	Nominal gross national product (Line 99b)
res	Austria	IFS	Foreign exchange reserves (Line 1d.d)
m	Austria	IFS	Narrow money (Line 34)
$\bar{g}$	Austria	IFS	Government consumption of goods and services (Line 99f)
r	Austria	IFS	Long-term government bond yield (Line 61)
C_P	Austria	IFS	Consumer prices (Line 64)
b	Austria	IFS	Central government debt (Line 88) less central bank claims on govt. (Line 12a)
s	Austria	IFS	Nominal capital stock, cumulated IFS private investment (Line 93e) from zero bench-mark in 1975. Depreciation was also set to zero.
GNP	Austria	IFS	Nominal gross national product (Line 99b)
res	Switzerland	IFS	Foreign exchange reserves (Line 1d.d)
m	Switzerland	IFS	Narrow money (Line 34)
$\bar{g}$	Switzerland	IFS	Government consumption of goods and services (Line 99f)
r	Switzerland	IFS	Long-term government bond yield (Line 61)
C_P	Switzerland	IFS	Consumer prices (Line 64)
b	Switzerland	IFS	Central government debt (Line 88) less central bank claims on govt. (Line 12a)
s	Switzerland	IFS	Nominal capital stock, cumulated IFS private investment (Line 93e) from zero bench-mark in 1975. Depreciation was also set to zero.

Variable	Country	Source	Comments
GNP	Switzerland	IFS	Nominal gross national product (Line 99b)
res	Sweden	IFS	Foreign exchange reserves (Line 1d.d)
m	Sweden	IFS	Narrow money (line 34) 1983–5 spliced using changes in domestic credit.
$\bar{g}$	Sweden	IFS	Government consumption of goods and services (Line 99f)
r	Sweden	IFS	Long-term government bond yield (Line 61)
C_P	Sweden	IFS	Consumer prices (Line 64)
b	Sweden	IFS	Central government debt (Line 88a and 88b) less central bank claims on govt. (Line 12a)
s	Sweden	IFS	Nominal capital stock, cumulated IFS private investment (Line 93e) from zero bench-mark in 1975. Depreciation was also set to zero.
GNP	Sweden	IFS	Nominal gross national product (Line 99b)
res	Netherlands	IFS	Foreign exchange reserves (Line 1d.d)
m	Netherlands	IFS	Narrow money (Line 34)
$\bar{g}$	Netherlands	IFS	Government consumption of goods and services (Line 99f)
r	Netherlands	IFS	Long-term goverment bond yield (Line 61)
C_P	Netherlands	IFS	Consumer prices (Line 64)
b	Netherlands	IFS	Central government debt (Line 88a and b) less central bank claims on govt. (Line 12a)
s	Netherlands	IFS	Nominal capital stock, cumulated IFS private investment (Line 93e) from zero bench-mark in 1975. Depreciation was also set to zero.
GNP	Netherlands	IFS	Nominal gross national product (Line 99b)
res	Belgium	IFS	Foreign exchange reserves (Line 1d.d)
m	Belgium	IFS	Narrow money (Line 34)
$\bar{g}$	Belgium	IFS	Government consumption of goods and services (Line 99f)
r	Belgium	IFS	Long-term government bond yield (Line 61)
C_P	Belgium	IFS	Consumer price (Line 64)
b	Belgium	IFS	Central government debt (Line 88) less central bank claims on govt. (Line 12a)
s	Belgium	IFS	Nominal capital stock, cumulated IFS private investment (Line 93e) from zero bench-mark in 1975). Depreciation was also set to zero.
GNP	Belgium	IFS	Nominal gross national product (Line 99b)

Source notation: **IFS** — International Monetary Fund, International Financial Statistics (the May 1987 tape); **CSO** — United Kingdom, Central Statistics Office, *Annual Abstract of Statistics*; **BB** — West Germany, Monthly *Bulletin* of the Bundesbank; **OECD** — OECD, *National Income Accounts*.

Appendix B

World capital accumulation

Introduction

This appendix extends the model of Chapter 5 to the case where the private sector holds a portfolio of assets that includes claims to real capital. The model is extremely simple, capturing only the demand side for financial capital. The firm and the real return on capital are not modelled explicitly; this is done by assuming that capital and bonds are perfect substitutes. First the required theoretical extensions are presented; then the results are provided; and finally, debt shock simulations are discussed.

The theory

The necessary theoretical extensions to the 'world' model presented in Chapter 5 are set out in equations (B.1) to (B.7):[1]

$$y = c + i + g \tag{B.1}$$

$$c = f(\omega, \bar{y}_d, r) \tag{B.2}$$

$$i = f(y, r) \tag{B.3}$$

$$\omega = m + b + s \tag{B.4}$$

$$m_s - m_d(r, y, \omega) = 0 \tag{B.5}$$

$$g = t + \dot{b} + \dot{m} \tag{B.6}$$

$$s_t = s_{t-1} + i_t \tag{B.7}$$

There are a number of key differences between this set-up and that in Chapter 5. The first is the separation of the consumption and investment functions. The investment function is based on standard accelerator arguments and has been kept as simple as possible, while still keeping the negative feedback role from interest rates to investment. The second is that the wealth identity now includes private holdings of capital, allowing changes in the capital stock to feed back onto the interest rate. Finally, a capital-accumulation equation has been added which defines the capital stock as a sum of past investment. There is no allowance for depreciation, although this would be a straightforward addition to make to the model.

The system consists of seven independent equations that can be solved for the seven endogenous variables.[2] As in the previous chapters, the approach taken to estimating the system involved substituting out equations that were not crucial to the issues at hand. Equation (B.5) was normalized on the interest rate, then income and wealth were substituted out using equations (B.1) to (B.4) leaving

$$r_t = \gamma_0 - \gamma_1 m_t + \gamma_2 b_t + \gamma_3 s_t + \gamma_4 g_t - \gamma_5 op_t.^3 \qquad (B.8)$$

The expected sign on the capital stock is positive because capital and bonds are perfect substitutes; a rise in the share of capital in the private sector's portfolio will only raise their demand for money, putting upward pressure on interest rates. Wealth effects in the consumption function reinforce the upward pressure on the interest rate. However, in a more fully specified model, where the interest rate was determined by the marginal productivity of capital, one might expect a rise in the capital stock to lower the marginal productivity of capital and the real rate of interest, at least in the long run. This is, in fact, the result suggested from the estimations.

The second equation to be estimated was derived from the capital accumulation equation (B.7). A functional relationship was obtained by substituting equations (B.1) to (B.4) for investment, giving

$$s_t = \delta_0 + \delta_1 m_t + \delta_2 b_t + \delta_3 g_t - \delta_4 r_t + \delta_5 s_{t-1}. \qquad (B.9)$$

The coefficients on all the policy variables should be positive, reflecting their positive impact on income or absorption. The interest rate, in contrast, should be negatively signed, reflecting its direct adverse effect on investment.

Estimation results

Table B.1 presents the estimated coefficients for the two equations derived above. The 'world' interest-rate equation is very similar to the fully reduced form presented in Chapter 5, performing marginally better with

Table B.1 'World' capital and interest-rate equations

Variable	Estimated coefficients						Statistics		
	m	b	g	op	r	$s\star$	$\bar{R}^2$	SE	DW
r	−83.846	20.792	−17.858	−0.048	–	−0.275	0.95	0.539	1.63
	(13.406)	(3.245)	(17.274)	(0.011)	(–)	(0.142)			
s	−0.318	0.035	0.247	–	−0.007	0.918	0.999	0.018	1.90
	(0.850)	(0.229)	(0.654)	(–)	(0.008)	(0.005)			

Note: $s\star$ represents current capital stock in the first equation and lagged capital in the second. Figures in parentheses are standard errors. Constant terms were estimated in all equations.

the inclusion of the capital stock. The capital stock coefficient is not quite significant and has the wrong sign. In fact, the size of the coefficient is so small that it suggests that the capital stock plays little role in the determination of short-run interest-rate fluctuations.

The capital accumulation equation is dominated by the lagged adjustment coefficient, pointing to very slow dynamics towards the long-run steady-state. Apart from the lagged adjustment term, only the interest rate shows any sign of being significant, but well below conventional significance levels. The poor results for this equation are not very surprising given the well-known difficulties of estimating investment or capital stock equations. The only comforting result was the negative sign on the real interest rate, something that is not always found in the literature.[4] In any case, for simulation purposes, the individual equation results are not necessarily a good indication of how a dynamic model will perform, which can only be ascertained from the solution to the entire system.

Model simulation

The two-equation system was solved over the sample period to test the model's ability to track data and to pick turning points. The results were very good. The RMSE on the real interest rate was 0.470, lower than the standard error of the single-equation estimation. The Thiel statistic, at 0.023, was also exceptionally low. The results for the capital stock were just as good, with the RMSE being roughly the same as the standard error of the single-equation estimation.

The model was next simulated into the future, holding exogenous variables constant, to create a baseline simulation. It was then possible to shock the 'world' debt stock and to track the dynamic response of both interest rates and the capital stock. The simulation results are presented in

Figure B.1 Interest-rate response

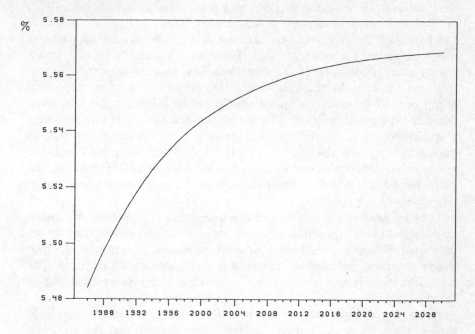

Figure B.2 Capital stock response

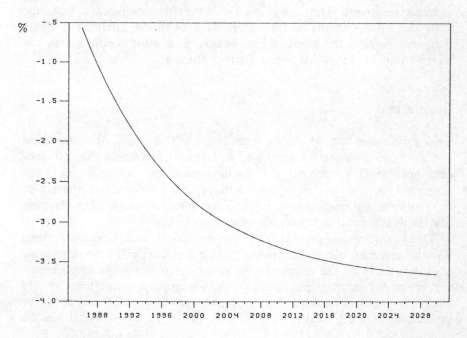

Figures B.1 and B.2. The policy experiment raises the 'world' debt-to-GNP ratio by 10 per cent (roughly three percentage points of trend GNP) in 1986 and holds it constant at this higher level.

The capital stock moves very little on impact. It initially falls by less then one percentage point of GNP. However, this builds up and within twenty years the increase in the debt stock has crowded out capital formation one for one. In the steady-state the multiplier is even more than minus one. These exact multipliers should not be taken too seriously given the data limitations involved; the aim of the simulations is rather to give a qualitative feel for the dynamic responses of financial markets to imposed changes in the 'world's' portfolio of assets. It should again be remembered that the actual rise in 'world' debt since the mid- to late 1970s has been nearly four times the size of the policy experiment undertaken above.

Looking next at the response of the interest rate, it is clear that much of the adjustment (upward as expected) to its long-run steady state occurs on impact. There is some further upward movement towards the long-run steady state, but this is small compared to the initial impact response. The full adjustment is very slow, taking more than thirty years according to the model.

Given the data limitations involved in estimating these functions, it should again be stressed that it is not being argued that the model is exactly replicating the response of the world economy to the actual debt expansion that has occurred. The results are only indicative of the likely dynamic responses. They hinge on two estimated coefficients: first, the large and highly significant coefficient on debt in the interest-rate equation; and second, the negative but weakly significant coefficient on the interest rate in the capital accumulation equation.

Conclusions

Two conclusions can be drawn from this analysis. First, the theoretical prediction of both the temporal and intertemporal models, that a higher debt stock will crowd out the capital stock one for one, has been supported by the 'world' model.[5] Second, the crowding-out appears to work primarily through higher real interest rates, although other channels (not explicitly modelled) may also be important.

These conclusions support both the monetarist and Keynesian views that the sustained non-cyclical use of deficit financing will have substantial negative effects on the economy, the point being that a closed economic system cannot improve permanently its consumption possibilities merely by borrowing from itself.[6] These results are in exact contrast to the predictions of the Ricardian Equivalence Theorem, which would see the private capital stock as being unaffected by the expansion of public sector debt.

Notes

1. Dots represent time derivatives and a bar over a variable indicates its long-run steady-state level. New notation includes private consumption (c), investment (i) and the stock of real capital (s)
2. The bond demand equation has been omitted by Walras's law.
3. The OPEC current account was included for the same reasons as set out in Chapter 5.
4. See, for example, Shapiro (1986), where the recent literature is discussed.
5. The theoretical predictions are, of course, only from those models that assume non-neutralities.
6. Monetarists would argue that benefits cannot even be gained from anti-cyclical deficit financing.

Bibliography

Aliber, Robert, 1973, 'The Interest Rate Parity Theorem: A Reinterpretation', *Journal of Political Economy*, 81, pp. 1451-9.

Amano, Akihiro, 1986, 'Exchange Rate Simulations: A Comparative Study', *European Economic Review*, 30, pp. 137-48.

Aoki, Masanao, 1983, *Dynamic Analysis of Open Economies* (New York Academic Press).

Argy, Victor, 1986, 'The Effects of Monetary and Fiscal Policy with Flexible Exchange Rates and Imperfect Asset Substitutability', International Economic Research Papers, no. 52.

Argy, Victor and Joanne Salop, 1979, 'Price and Output Effects of Monetary and Fiscal Policy under Flexible Exchange Rates', *IMF Staff Papers*, 26, pp. 224-56.

Aschauer, David and Jeremy Greenwood, 1985, 'Macroeconomic Effects of Fiscal Policy', *Carnegie-Rochester Conference Series on Public Policy*, 38, pp. 91-138.

Atkinson, Paul and Jean-Claude Chouraqui, 1985, 'Real Interest Rates and the Prospects for Durable Growth', OECD Working Papers, no. 21, May.

Ballassa, Bela, 1964, 'The Purchasing Power Parity Doctrine: A Reappraisal', *Journal of Political Economy*, 72, pp. 275-99.

Barro, Robert, 1974, 'Are Government Bonds Net Wealth?', *Journal of Political Economy*, 82, pp. 1095-1117.

Barro, Robert, 1979, 'On the Determination of Public Debt', *Journal of Political Economy*, 87, pp. 941-71.

Barro, Robert, 1983, 'Real Determinants of Real Exchange Rates', mimeo, University of Chicago.

Barro, Robert, 1987a, 'Government Spending, Interest Rates, Prices and Budget Deficits in the United Kingdom 1701-1918', *Journal of Monetary Economics*, 20, pp. 221-47.

Barro, Robert, 1987b, 'The Economic Effects of Budget Deficits and Government Spending', *Journal of Monetary Economics*, 20. pp. 191-3.

Blanchard, Oliver, 1985, 'Debt, Deficits and Finite Horizons', *Journal of Political Economy*, 93, pp. 223-47.

Blanchard, Oliver and Rudiger Dornbusch, 1984, 'US Deficits, the Dollar and Europe', *Banca Nazionale del Lavoro Quarterly Review*, March, pp. 89-113.

Blanchard, Oliver and Lawrence Summers, 1984, 'Perspectives on High World Real Interest Rates', *Brookings Papers on Economic Activity*, no. 2, pp. 273-324.

Boskin, Michael and Laurence Kotlikoff, 1985, 'Public Debt and US Savings: A New Test of the Neutrality Hypothesis', *Carnegie-Rochester Conference Series on Public Policy*, 23, pp. 55-86.

Branson, William, 1985, 'The Dynamic Interaction of Exchange Rates and Trade Flows', NBER Working Paper, no. 1780, December.

Branson, William, 1986, 'The Limits of Monetary Coordination as Exchange Rate Policy', *Brookings Papers on Economic Activity*, 1, pp. 175-94.

Branson, William *et al.*, 1977, 'Exchange Rates in the Short-Run', *European Economic Review*, 10, pp. 303-24.

Branson, William *et al.*, 1985, 'Expansionary Fiscal Policy and the Recession of 1982', NBER Working Paper, no. 1784, December.

Branson, William and Willem Buiter, 1983, 'Monetary and Fiscal Policy with Flexible Exchange Rates', in Jagdeep Bhandari and Bluford Putnam (eds) *The International Transmission of Economic Disturbances Under Flexible Exchange Rates*, Cambridge MA, MIT Press.

Bruce, Neil and Douglas Purvis, 1976, 'The Specification and Influence of Goods and Factor Markets in the Open Economy Macromodel', in Ronald Jones and Peter Kenen (eds), *Handbook of International Economics* (Amsterdam, North Holland).

Bruno, Michael, 1976, 'The Two-Sector Open Economy and the Real Exchange Rate', *American Economic Review*, 66, pp. 566–77.

Buchanan, J., 1958, *Principles of Public Debt* Homewood, Il., Irwin.

Buiter, Willem, 1981, 'Time Preference and International Lending and Borrowing in an Overlapping-Generations Model', *Journal of Political Economy*, 89, pp. 769–97.

Buiter, Willem, 1983, 'Measurement of the Public Sector Deficit and its Implications for Policy Evaluation and Design', *IMF Staff Papers*, 30, pp. 306–49.

Buiter, Willem, 1985, 'A Guide to Public Sector Debt and Deficits', *Economic Policy*, 1, pp. 14–79.

Buiter, Willem, 1986, 'Structural and Stabilization Aspects of Fiscal and Financial Policy in the Dependent Economy', NBER Working Paper, no. 2023.

Camen, Ulrich and Hans Genberg, 1986, 'Under and Over-Valuation of Currencies: Theory, Measurement and Policy Implications', mimeo, January, Graduate Institute of International Studies, Geneva.

Carmichael, Jeffrey, 1982, 'On Barro's Theorem of Debt Neutrality: The Irrelevance of Net Wealth', *American Economic Review*, 72, pp. 202–13.

Carmichael, Jeffrey, 1984, 'Pitfalls in Testing the Ricardian Equivalence Theorem', Reserve Bank of Australia, mimeo.

Chouraqui, Jean-Claude *et al.*, 1986, 'Public Debt in a Medium-Term Context and its Implications for Fiscal Policy', OECD Working Paper.

Christ, Carl, 1979, 'On Fiscal and Monetary Policies and the Government Budget Constraint', *American Economic Review*, 69, pp. 539–52.

Clements, Ken and Jacob Frenkel, 1980, 'Exchange Rates, Money, and Relative Prices', *Journal of International Economics*, 10, pp. 249–62.

Cohen, Daniel, 1985, 'How to Evaluate the Solvency of an Indebted Nation', *Economic Forum*, 1, pp. 140–67.

Corden, Max, 1986, 'Fiscal Policies, Current Accounts and Real Exchange Rates: In Search of a Logic of International Policy Coordination', *Weltwirtschaftliches Archiv*, 122, pp. 423–38.

Cumby, Robert and Maurice Obstfeld, 1984, 'International Interest Rate and Price Level Linkages under Flexible Exchange rates' in John Bilson and Richard Marston (eds), *Exchange Rate Theory and Practice* (Chicago, Chicago University Press).

De Grauwe, Paul and Theo Peeters (eds), 1983, *Exchange Rates in Multicountry Econometric Models* (London, Macmillan).

Devereux, Michael and Douglas Purvis, 1984, 'Fiscal Policy and the Real Exchange Rate', Queens Discussion Paper no. 593, December.

Diamond, Paul, 1965, 'National Debt in a Neo-Classical Growth Model', *American Economic Review*, 55, pp. 1126–50.

Dooley, Michael and Peter Isard, 1980, 'Capital Controls, Political Risk, and Deviations from Interest Parity', *Journal of Political Economy*, 88, pp. 370–84.

Dornbusch, Rudiger, 1976, 'Expectations and Exchange Rate Dynamics', *Journal of Political Economy*, 84, pp. 1161–76.

Dornbusch, Rudiger, 1980, 'Exchange Rate Economics: Where Do We Stand?', *Brookings Papers on Economic Activity*, 1, pp. 143–85.

Dornbusch, Rudiger, 1983, 'Real Interest Rates, Home Goods, and Optimal External Borrowing', *Journal of Political Economy*, 91, pp. 141–53.

Dornbusch, Rudiger, 1987, 'Exchange Rates and Prices', *American Economic Review*, 77, pp. 93–106.

Dornbusch, Rudiger and Stanley Fischer, 1980, 'Exchange Rates and Current Accounts', *American Economic Review*, 70, pp. 960–77.

Echols, Michael and Jan Elliot, 1976, 'Rational Expectations in a Disequilibrium Model of the Term Structure', *American Economic Review*, 66, pp. 28–44.

Eichengreen, Barry and Charles Wyplosz, 1986, 'The Economic Consequences of the Franc Poincaré', INSEAD Working papers, No. 86/26, September.

Eisner, Robert and Paul Piper, 1984, 'A New View of the Federal Debt and Budget Deficits', *American Economic Review*, 74, pp. 11–29.

Evans, Paul, 1985, 'Do Large Deficits Produce High Interest Rates?', *American Economic Review*, 75, pp. 68–87.

Evans, Paul, 1986, 'Is the Dollar High Because of Large Budget Deficits?', *Journal of Monetary Economics*, 18, pp. 227–49.

Evans, Paul, 1987a, 'Interest Rates and Expected Future Budget Deficits in the United States', *Journal of Political Economy*, 95, pp. 34–58.

Evans, Paul, 1987b, 'Do Budget Deficits Raise Nominal Interest Rates? Evidence From Six Countries', *Journal of Monetary Economics*, 20, pp. 281–300.

Fair, Ray, 1984, *Specification, Estimation, and Analysis of Macroeconomic Models* (Cambridge, MA, Harvard University Press).

Fair, Ray, 1986, 'Interest Rate and Exchange Rate Determination', NBER Working Paper, no. 2105.

Feldstein, Martin, 1982, 'Government Deficits and Aggregate Demand', *Journal of Monetary Economics*, 9, pp. 1–20.

Feldstein, Martin, 1983, 'Domestic Savings and International Capital Movements in the Long and the Short Run', *European Economic Review*, 21, pp. 129–151.

Feldstein, Martin, 1986a, 'The Budget Deficit and the Dollar', NBER Working Paper, no. 1898, April.

Feldstein, Martin, 1986b, 'Budget Deficits, Tax Rules, and Real Interest Rates', NBER Working Paper, no. 1970, July.

Feldstein, Martin and Otto Eckstein, 1970, 'The Fundamental Determinants of the Interest Rate', *Review of Economics and Statistics*, 52, pp. 363–75.

Feldstein, Martin and Charles Horioka, 1980, 'Domestic Savings and International Capital Flows', *Economic Journal*, 90, pp. 314–29.

Fischer, Stanley, 1987, 'International Macroeconomic Policy Coordination', NBER Working Paper, no. 2244, May.

Frankel, Jeffrey, 1979, 'On the Mark: A Theory of Floating Exchange Rates Based on Real Interest Differentials', *American Economic Review*, 69, pp. 610–22.

Frankel, Jeffrey, 1983, 'Monetary and Portfolio-Balance Models of Exchange Rate Determination', in Jagdeep Bhandari and Bluford Putnam (eds), *Economic Interdependence and Flexible Exchange Rates* (Cambridge MA, MIT Press).

Frankel, Jeffrey, 1985, 'International Capital Mobility and Crowding Out in the US Economy: Imperfect Integration of Financial Markets or of Goods Markets?', paper presented to the Federal Reserve Bank of St. Louis conference on 'How Open Is the US Economy?', October.

Frankel, Jeffrey, 1986, 'Conflicting International Macro Models: Sources, and

Implications For Policy Coordination', paper presented to Brookings Conference on 'Empirical Macroeconomics for Interdependent Economies', Washington, DC, March.

Frankel, Jeffrey and Kenneth Froot 1987, 'Using Survey Data to Test Standard Propositions Regarding Exchange Rate Expectations', *American Economic Review*, 77, pp. 133–47.

Frenkel, Jacob and Assaf Razin, 1985, 'Government Spending, Debt, and International Economic Interdependence', *Economic Journal*, 95, pp. 619–36.

Frenkel, Jacob and Assaf Razin, 1986a, 'Fiscal Policies in the World Economy', *Journal of Political Economy*, 94, pp. 564–94.

Frenkel, Jacob and Assaf Razin, 1986b, 'Real Exchange Rates, Interest Rates and Fiscal Policies', *Economic Studies Quarterly*, 37, pp. 99–113.

Frenkel, Jacob and Assaf Razin, 1986c, 'Fiscal Policies and Real Exchange Rates in the World Economy', NBER Working Paper, no. 2065.

Frenkel, Jacob and Assaf Razin, 1987, *Fiscal Policies and the World economy: An Intertemporal Approach* (Boston, MIT Press).

Friedman, Benjamin, 1978, 'Crowding Out or Crowding in? Economic Consequences of Financing Government Deficits', *Brookings Papers on Economic Activity*, 3, pp. 593–654.

Friedman, Benjamin, 1986, 'Implications of the United States Net Capital Inflow', NBER Working Paper, No. 1804, January.

Friedman, Milton, 1972, 'Comments on the Critics', *Journal of Political Economy*, 80, pp. 906–45.

Genberg, Hans, 1978, 'Purchasing Power Parity under Fixed and Flexible Exchange Rates', *Journal of International Economics*, 8, pp. 247–67.

Genberg, Hans, 1984, 'On Choosing the Right Rules for Exchange-Rate Management', *World Economy*, 7, pp. 391–406.

Genberg, Hans and Henryk Kierzkowski, 1979, 'Impact and Long-Run Effects of Economic Disturbances in a Dynamic Model of Exchange Rate Determination', *Weltwirtschaftliches Archiv*, 140, pp. 603–28.

Girton, Lance and Dale Henderson, 1976, 'Financial Capital Movements and Central Bank Behaviour in a Two-Country Short-Run Portfolio-Balance Model', *Journal of Monetary Economics*, 2, pp. 33–61.

Haas, Richard and Paul Masson, 1986, 'MINIMOD: Specification and Simulation Results', *IMF Staff Papers*, 33, pp. 722–67.

Hamada, Kochi, 1984, 'Strategic Aspects of International Fiscal Interdependence', mimeo, February, University of Tokyo.

Hansson, Ingemar and Charles Stuart, 1986, 'The Fisher Hypothesis and International Capital Markets', *Journal of Political Economy*, 94, pp. 1330–7.

Helkie, William and Peter Hooper, 1987, 'The US External Deficit in the 1980s: An Empirical Analysis', International Finance Discussion Papers, no. 304.

Hoelscher, Gregory, 1986, 'New Evidence on Deficits and Interest Rates', *Journal of Money, Credit and Banking*, 18, pp. 1–17.

Holtham Gerald, 1986, 'Exchange Rates in the OECD Interlink Model', *European Economic Review*, 30, pp. 199–235.

Hooper, Peter, 1985, 'International Repercussions of the US Budget Deficit', Brookings Discussion Papers in International Economics, no. 27.

Hooper, Peter, 1986, 'Exchange Rate Simulation Properties of the MCM', *European Economic Review*, 30, pp. 171–98.

Hooper, Peter and John Morton, 1982, 'Fluctuations in the Dollar: A Model of Nominal and Real Exchange Rate Determination', *Journal of International Money and Finance*, 1, pp. 39–56.

Isard, Peter, 1977, 'How Far Can We Push the Law of One Price?', *American Economic Review*, 26, pp. 942-8.

Isard, Peter, 1983, 'An Accounting Framework and Some Issues for Modelling How Exchange Rates Respond to the News' in Jacob Frenkel (ed.), *Exchange Rates and International Macroeconomics* (Chicago, NBER and University of Chicago Press).

Isard, Peter, 1987, 'Lessons from Empirical Models of Exchange Rates', *IMF Staff Papers*, 34, pp. 1-28.

Kaneko, Takafumi and Norikazu Yasuhara, 1986, 'Exchange Rate Simulations with the EPA World Economic Model', *European Economic Review*, 30, pp. 237-59.

Katseli, Louka, 1983, 'Real Exchange Rates in the 1970s' in John Bilson and Richard Marston (eds), *Exchange Rate Theory and Practice* (Chicago, University of Chicago Press).

Knight, Malcolm and Paul Masson, 1985, 'Fiscal Policies, Net Savings and Real Exchange Rates: United States, Japan and the Federal Republic of Germany', paper presented to the NBER conference on 'International Aspects of Fiscal Policies', Cambridge, MA, December.

Kochin, Levis, 1974, 'Are Future Taxes Anticipated by Consumers?', *Journal of Money, Credit and Banking*, 6, pp. 385-94.

Kole, Linda, 1985, 'Expansionary Fiscal Policy and International Interdependence', paper presented to the NBER Conference on 'International Aspects of Fiscal Policies', Cambridge, MA, December.

Kormendi, Roger, 1983, 'Government Debt, Government Spending, and Private Sector Behaviour', *American Economic Review*, 73, pp. 994-1010.

Koskela, Errki and Matti Viren, 1983, 'National Debt Neutrality: Some International Evidence', *Kyklos*, 36, pp. 575-88.

Krugman, Paul, 1986, 'Is the Strong Dollar Sustainable?', paper presented to Federal Reserve Bank of Kansas City Conference.

Laursen, S. and Lloyd Metzler, 1950, 'Flexible Exchange Rates and the Theory of Employment', *Review of Economics and Statistics*, 32, pp, 281-99.

Lucas, Robert, 1982, 'Interest Rates and Currency Prices in a Two-Country World', *Journal of Monetary Economics*, 10, pp. 355-60.

Makin, John, 1983, 'Real Interest, Money Surprises, Anticipated Inflation and Fiscal Deficits', *Review of Economics and Statistics*, 65, pp. 374-84.

Mankiw, Gregory, 1986, 'Government Purchases and Real Interest Rates', NBER Working Paper, no. 2009, August.

Marston, Richard, 1985, 'Stabilization Policies in Open Economies' in Ronald Jones and Peter Kenen (eds) *Handbook of International Economics*, Vol. 2 (Amsterdam, North Holland).

Mascaro, Angelo and Allen Meltzer, 1983, 'Long and Short-term Interest Rates in a Risky World', *Journal of Monetary Economics*, 12, pp. 485-518.

Masson, Paul, 1986, 'The Dynamics of a Two-Country Minimodel under Rational Expectations', paper presented to a conference on 'Modelling Dynamic Systems', June.

McKinnon, Ronald, 1984, 'An International Standard for Monetary Stabilization', *Policy Analysis in International Economics*, 7 (Washington Institute for International Economics).

Meese, Richard and Kenneth Rogoff, 1983a, 'Empirical Exchange Rate Models of the Seventies: Do They Fit Out-of-sample?', *Journal of International Economics*, 14, pp. 3-24.

Meese, Richard and Kenneth Rogoff, 1983b, 'The Out-of-sample Failure of

Empirical Exchange Rate Models: Sampling Error or Misspecification?', in Jacob Frenkel (ed.), *Exchange Rates and International Macroeconomics* (Chicago, NBER and University of Chicago Press).

Meese, Richard and Kenneth Rogoff, 1985, 'Was It Real' The Exchange Rate–Interest Rate Differential Relation, 1973–1984', NBER Working Paper, no. 1732.

Merrick, John and Allen Saunders, 1986, 'International Expected Real Interest Rates', *Journal of Monetary Economics*, 18, pp. 313–22.

Metzler, Lloyd, 1951, 'Wealth, Savings, and the Rate of Interest', *Journal of Political Economy*, 59, pp. 93–116.

Minford, Patrick, 1985, 'The Effects of American Policies — A New Classical Interpretation' in Willem Buiter and Richard Marston (eds) *International Economic Policy Coordination* (Cambridge, Cambridge University Press).

Mishkin, Frederick, 1982, 'The Real Interest Rate: A Multi-Country Empirical Study', mimeo, January.

Modigliani, Franco, 1961, 'Long-run Implications of Alternative Fiscal Policies and the Burden of National Debt', *Economic Journal*, 71, pp. 730–55.

Mundell, Robert, 1968, *International Economics* (New York, Macmillan).

Mussa, Michael, 1979, 'Macroeconomic Interdependence and the Exchange Rate Regime' in Rudiger Dornbusch and Jacob Frenkel (eds), *International Economic Policy: Theory and Practice* (Baltimore, MD, John Hopkins University Press).

Mussa, Michael, 1986, 'Nominal Exchange Rate Regimes and the Behaviour of Real Exchange Rates: Evidence and Implications', *Carnegie-Rochester Conference Series on Public Policy*, 25, pp. 117–213.

Mutoh, Taka, 1985, 'The Equivalence of the Burden of Internal and External Public Debt', *Economic Letters*, 17, pp. 369–72.

Neary, Peter and Douglas Purvis, 1983, 'Real Adjustment and Exchange Rate Dynamics' in Jacob Frenkel (ed.), *Exchange Rates and International Macroeconomics* (Chicago, University of Chicago Press).

Obstfeld, Maurice, 1981, 'Macroeconomic Policy, Exchange Rate Dynamics, and Optimal Asset Accumulation', *Journal of Political Economy*, 89, pp. 1142–61.

Obstfeld, Maurice, 1986, 'Capital Mobility in the World Economy: Theory and Measurement', *Carnegie-Rochester Conference Series on Public Policy*, 24, pp. 55–103.

Officer, Lawrence, 1976, 'The Purchasing Power Parity Theory of Exchange Rates: A Review Article', *IMF Staff Papers*, 23, pp. 1–60.

Ott, Mack, 1987, 'The Dollar's Effective Exchange Rate: Assessing the Impact of Alternative Weighting Schemes', *Federal Reserve Bank of St. Louis Review*, 68, pp. 5–14.

Oudiz, Gilles and Jeffrey Sachs, 1984, 'Macroeconomic Policy Coordination Among the Industrialized Countries', *Brookings Papers on Economic Activity*, 1, pp. 1–75.

Pauly, Peter and Christian Petersen, 1986, 'Exchange Rate Responses in the LINK System', *European Economic Review*, 30, pp. 149–70.

Penati, Allesandro, 1983, 'Expansionary Fiscal Policy and the Exchange Rate', *IMF Staff Papers*, 30, pp. 542–69.

Persson, Torsten, 1985, 'Deficits and Intergenerational Welfare in Open Economies', *Journal of International Economics*, 19, pp. 67–84.

Persson, Torsten and Lars Svensson, 1985, 'Current Account Dynamics and the Terms of Trade: Harberger–Laursen–Metzler Two Generations Later', *Journal of Political Economy*, 93, pp. 43–65.

Pindyck, Robert and Daniel Rubinfeld, 1981, *Econometric Models and Economic Forecasting* (New York, McGraw-Hill, International Edition).

Plosser, Charles, 1982, 'Government Financing Decisions and Asset Returns', *Journal of Monetary Economics*, 9, pp. 325–52.

Plosser, Charles, 1987, 'Fiscal Policy and the Term Structure', *Journal of Monetary Economics*, 20, pp. 343–67.

Poterba, James and Lawrence Summers, 1987, 'Finite Lifetimes and the Effects of Budget Deficits on National Saving', *Journal of Monetary Economics*, 20, pp. 369–91.

Price, Robert and Patrice Muller, 1984, 'Structural Budget Deficits and Fiscal Stance', OECD Working Paper, no. 15, July.

Purvis, Douglas, 1985, 'Public Sector Deficits, International Capital Movements, and the Domestic Economy: The Medium-term is the Message', *Canadian Journal of Economics*, 18, pp. 723–42.

Roll, Richard, 'Violations of Purchasing Power Parity and Their Implications for Efficient International Commodity Markets' in M. Sarnat and P. Szego (eds), *International Finace and Trade* (Cambridge, MA, Ballinger Publishing Co.).

Sachs, Jeffrey, 1985, 'The Dollar and the Policy Mix: 1985', *Brookings Papers on Economic Activity*, no. 1, pp. 117–97.

Sachs, Jeffrey and Charles Wyplosz, 1984, 'Real Exchange Rate Effects of Fiscal Policy', NBER Working Paper, no. 1255, January.

Sargent, Thomas, 1969, 'Commodity Price Expectations and the Interest Rate', *Quarterly Journal of Economics*, 83, pp. 325–52.

Sargent, Thomas and Neil Wallace, 1982, 'Some Unpleasant Monetarist Arithmetic', *Federal Reserve Bank of Minneapolis Quarterly Review*, Winter, pp. 15–31.

Schinasi, Gary, 1986, 'International Comparisons of Fiscal Policy: The OECD and the IMF Measures of Fiscal Impulse', International Finance Discussion Papers, no. 274, February.

Seater, John, 1982, 'Are Future Taxes Discounted?', *Journal of Money, Credit and Banking*, 14, pp. 376–89.

Seater, John, 1985, 'Does Government Debt Matter? A Review', *Journal of Monetary Economics*, 16, pp. 121–31.

Shapiro, Matthew, 1986, 'Investment, Output, and the Cost of Capital', *Brookings Papers on Economic Activity*, 1, pp. 111–50.

Stevens, Guy, *et al.*, 1984, *The US Economy in an Interdependent World, A Multicountry Model*, (Washington, DC, Federal Reserve System).

Stockman, Alan, 1980, 'A Theory of Exchange Rate Determination', *Journal of Political Economy*, 88, pp. 673–97.

Stockman, Alan, 1983, 'Real Exchange Rates under Alternative Exchange-Rate Systems', *Journal of International Money and Finance*, 2, pp. 147–66.

Tanzi, Vito, 1985, 'Fiscal Deficits and Interest Rates in the United States: An Empirical Analysis', *IMF Staff Papers*, 32, pp. 551–76.

Theil, Henri, 1961, *Economic Forecasts and Policy* (Amsterdam, North Holland).

Thursby, Jerry, 1987, 'OLS or GLS in the Presence of Specification Error?', *Journal of Econometrics*, 35, pp. 359–74.

Tobin, James, 1969, 'A General Equilibrium Approach to Monetary Theory', *Journal of Money, Credit and Banking*, 1, pp. 15–29.

Turnovsky, Stephen, 1986, 'Monetary and Fiscal Policy under Perfect Foresight: A Symmetric Two-country Analysis', *Economica*, 210, pp. 139–58.

United States Treasury Department, 1984, *The Effects of Deficits on Prices of Financial Assets* (Washington, DC, US Government Printing Office), March.

Van Wijnbergen, Sweder, 1984, 'On Fiscal Deficits, The Real Exchange Rate and the World Rate of Interest', CEPR Discussion Paper, No. 21, July.

Van Wijnbergen, Sweder, 1985, 'Fiscal Deficits, Exchange Rate Crises and Inflation', CEPR Discussion Paper, no. 87, December.

Van Wijnbergen, Sweder, 1986a, 'On Fiscal Deficits, The Real Exchange Rate and the World Rate of Interest', *European Economic Review*, 30, pp. 1013–23.

Van Wijnbergen, Sweder, 1986b, 'Interdependence Revisited: A Developing Country Perspective on Macroeconomic Management and Trade Policy in the Industrial World', *Economic Policy*, 1, pp. 82–137.

Wallis, Kenneth and John Whitley, 1986, 'Long-run Properties of Large-scale Macroeconomic Models', paper presented at a conference on 'Modelling Dynamic Systems', June.

Weiller, Kenneth, 1984, 'Reduced Form Evidence on the Effects of Fiscal Policy on Real Exchange Rates', mimeo, November.

Williamson, John, 1985, 'The Exchange Rate System', *Policy Analysis in International Economics*, 5.

Yotsuzuka, Toshiki, 1987, 'Ricardian Equivalence in the Presence of Capital Market Imperfections', *Journal of Monetary Economics*, 20, pp. 411–36.

Index

absorption variables 89, 91–2
  see also variables
accounting
  intertemporal 16–18
adaptive expectations assumptions 94
  see also expectations, variables
add factors 82
adjustment paths 59
aggregation problems 63, 71, 73, 76
aggregation techniques 92, 93
ambiguity 87–8
anti-cyclical variations 15
  see also cyclical variations
asset substitutability 55, 63, 65
  imperfect 31, 40–3
  perfect 40
asset-market integration 50, 91
assets *see* financial assets
asymmetries 2

banks *see* central banks
Barro's theory 20, 91
Blanchard models 22, 25, 26
  see also models
bonds *see* government bonds
Branson models 41, 42
  see also models
budget constraints 17, 39, 41–2, 68, 86
budget deficits 1–2, 30–1, 39
  United States 1–2, 9–10, 15, 55–6,
  59–60, 81, 104–9

capital accumulation equations 66, 85,
  130–5
  see also equations
capital markets 3, 124
  see also financial markets
capital mobility 2, 35–7, 65, 70–1, 76–8
  zero 35, 37, 70
Carmichael models 21
  see also models
central banks 117
closed economies 49
closed economy models 2, 16–23, 27–8, 30,
  31–5, 44–5, 53–4, 65
  see also models
communications technology 1, 3
consumer durables 75–6
consumer prices 4, 37
  see also prices

consumers 22, 25, 33, 37
  see also individual taxation
consumption functions 50–1
co-ordinated fiscal policies 120–3, 124
cross-country linkages 54, 71
  see also linkages
crowding-out 2, 30
cyclical variations 4, 30–1
  anti-cyclical 15
  equilibrium 31, 34, 38, 39–40, 86–7

data collection 92–3, 126–9
debt neutrality 2, 16, 18–21
debt repayment 21
deficits *see* budget deficits
dependent variables 53
  see also variables
depreciation 55
Diamond models 22, 25–6
  see also models
disposable wages 33–4
  see also wages
Dornbusch models 38–9, 86–7
  see also models
Durbin-Watson statistics 71, 74, 76, 95, 97
  see also statistics
dynamic Mundell-Fleming models 38–40
  see also Mundell-Fleming models

econometrics 2
  see also theoretical economies
empirical models 15–16, 49–63, 65–79,
  81–113, 117–25
  see also models
endogenous variables 89, 93
  see also variables
EPA models 59
  see also models
equations 82, 88–9
  capital accumulation 66, 85, 130–5
  errors 95
  exchange-rate 54–7
  interest-rate 51–4, 68–71, 40–1
  linearization 89
  normalization 89
  reduced form 54, 66, 68–71
equilibrium 31, 34, 38, 39–40, 86–7
  see also cyclical variations
Equivalence Theorem *see* Riccardian
  Equivalence Theorem